THE
FUNDAMENTALS
OF INTERIOR
DESIGN

BLOOMSBURY VISUAL ARTS
Bloomsbury Publishing Plc
50 Bedford Square, London, WC1B 3DP, UK
1385 Broadway, New York, NY 10018, USA

BLOOMSBURY, BLOOMSBURY VISUAL ARTS and the Diana logo are
trademarks of Bloomsbury Publishing Plc

First edition published in Great Britain by AVA Publishing SA 2009
Second edition published by Fairchild Books 2015
Reprinted 2016, 2017, 2018
This edition published by Bloomsbury Visual Arts 2018

A catalogue record for this book is available from the British Library.

The Library of Congress has cataloged the AVA edition as follows:
Dodsworth, Simon.
The fundamentals of interior design / Simon Dodsworth and Stephen
Anderson. — Second edition. pages cm. — (Fundamentals)
"First published 2009."
Includes bibliographical references and index.
ISBN: 978-1-4725-2853-7 (paperback)
1. Interior decoration. I. Title.
NK2110.D63 2015
729—dc23
2014030627

ISBN: PB: 978-1-3501-0656-7
       ePDF: 978-1-4725-2184-2
       eBook: 978-1-4742-3934-9

Series: Fundamentals

Typeset by Atelier David Smith, Dublin, Ireland
Printed and bound in India

To find out more about our authors and books visit
www.bloomsbury.com and sign up for our newsletters.

THE
FUNDAMENTALS
OF INTERIOR
DESIGN

SECOND EDITION

Simon Dodsworth
with Stephen Anderson

BLOOMSBURY VISUAL ARTS
LONDON • NEW YORK • OXFORD • NEW DELHI • SYDNEY

Contents

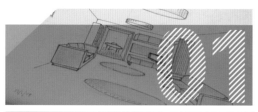

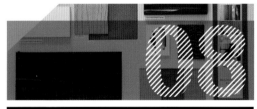

Introduction

—

To be creative is part of the human psyche. It is one of those traits that sets us apart from other animal species, and we have practiced it for millennia. Even when our prime need was to find food and shelter, we felt a desire to leave our mark on the environments that we inhabited. Whether this was to satisfy some deep spiritual calling, or a method of passing on vital knowledge to fellow group members, or whether it was simply a way for an individual to satisfy an urge to leave his mark for future generations, we will never know. For just as long, people have turned inquisitive minds to ways of solving problems and dealing with the issues that have faced them in the struggle to survive: problems such as how to work more efficiently, how to live more comfortably, and how to be safe from danger.

Today, these primitive and fundamental indicators of human nature may be expressed in more sophisticated and developed ways, but the primal simplicity of our human desire to make a "better" and more comfortable world for ourselves is evidenced through, among other things, how we organize the spaces that we inhabit and the aesthetic that we make for them.

As we have become more affluent and blessed with more leisure time, style has become more important to us, and it is something with which we want to imbue our homes. But "style" is a very personal notion, so why should anyone look to employ someone else, such as an interior designer, to tell them what is right? Why, for that matter, should you as a designer presume to impose your ideas upon a space that isn't your own? The answer is this: interior design is about so much more than "what looks right." It is about taking a holistic view of the way individuals use and enjoy the spaces they inhabit. It is about finding and creating a cohesive answer to a set of problems and dressing the solution so as to unify and strengthen our experience of the space. Many people understand this, and they also understand that they do not have the necessary insight, skills, and intellectual grasp of the issues to tackle the job themselves. And so there is the need for professional interior designers.

What is interior design?

—

Good interior design adds a new dimension to a space. It can increase our efficiency in the way we go about our daily lives, and it adds depth, understanding, and meaning to the built environment. Thoughtful and well-crafted design makes a space easier to understand, and experiencing such a space lifts the spirit, too. It is, therefore, not just about the aesthetic; it is a practical and philosophical discipline. Beautiful spaces show a logical and rational questioning of the status quo and can be an honest attempt to find new and exciting ways to lead our lives. In some areas of design, such as hospitality design (the design of bars, restaurants, hotels, etc.), the designer's work can play a large part in creating a successful business for the owners.

There is often confusion between the terms "architect," "interior architect," "interior designer," and "interior decorator." In truth, the distinctions between these professions are not absolute, and there is a great deal of overlap. Where boundaries are drawn depends upon several factors. In a professional sense, it may well come down to a matter of which country the designer is working in (or perhaps more properly, which regulatory system the designer is working under). Though not definitive, the explanations below give an indication of the different roles and responsibilities of those whose work involves the design of habitable space.

Architects define the volumes (spaces) that combine to make up a building through the careful composition of planes (walls, floors, ceilings). They are trained to design structures from scratch, though they may well be involved with the refurbishment of an existing structure. They will take intellectual and practical considerations into account, and the building design will be informed by its location. Some architects will limit their involvement to this, while others will also consider furniture and fittings in addition to materials and finishes.

Interior architects generally focus their skills on existing structures and repurposing them to suit new functions, and as such they will often see their work as a sustainable way of dealing with the built environment. They will pay a great deal of regard to the previous life of a building and usually allow this knowledge to provide some connection between the building and their newly created interior.

Interior decorators generally work with clients who want to change the look and feel of a space without resorting to major structural change or intervention. Through the use of color, light, and surface finishes, they will transform the space, perhaps making it suitable to function in a different way from which it was originally designed. Their work may well be informed less by the previous history of the building or its location.

Interior design spans the ground between interior architecture and interior decoration. The scope of the projects undertaken by interior designers will vary, from the purely decorative to ones where a great deal of structural change is required to meet the brief. Whatever the scope, interior designers will approach a project with a desire for interpretation and meaning within their work that will generally set them apart from interior decorators. An interior designer will competently handle the space planning and creation of decorative schemes at the same time as considering major structural changes. However, being trained in only the basics of structure, designers will recognize when to call on other professionals (such as structural engineers) to ensure that their proposals are legal and safe. In fact, architects, interior architects, interior designers, and interior decorators will all call on other specialists where appropriate to help fully realize their ideas.

7

Why become an interior designer?

—

Being an interior designer puts you in a privileged position. You are trusted by the client, and in the case of commissions by private clients, you have intimate access to their homes and way of life. You are given freedom to create spaces that will become an everyday part of their lives. You can propose radical planning solutions that may overturn preconceptions. According to the budget, you will source and curate all the elements that make up the interior space. You can select beautiful pieces of furniture, interesting and unusual finishes, and color schemes that together create drama, serenity, or whatever other mood the client wants for their space.

For a creative personality all of this is satisfying in itself, but the problems that the global community will face through the coming decades offer lots of opportunities to expand our creativity further. Climate change, population growth, and unsustainable consumption are causing problems that need to be addressed, and the solutions are almost all to do with the way that we lead our lives. Current ways of working and living will change, and whether these changes turn out to be sudden and dramatic, or slower and more subtle, changes in lifestyle will mean that designers are required to navigate new landscapes and propose alternative routes for clients to allow them to meet their commitments as part of a new global, responsible society while still maintaining a sense of well-being derived from their immediate surroundings.

As well as these changes, there is a growing acceptance that the current condition of public and private spaces does not facilitate their use equally by all members of society. "Inclusive design" attempts to answer this by considering the needs of all people during the design process; that is, anyone and everyone who may have call to use the space—including children, the elderly, those carrying heavy or awkward loads, and so on.

0.1

Interior design projects require many different skills from the design team to make spaces that work practically and aesthetically. Conran & Partners designed the Kuryakin Meeting Room in the South Place Hotel, London, UK. The focal point is a scarlet lacquered table surrounded by red leather chairs; above it hangs a circular chandelier that echoes the shape of the table. Here, ideas about space planning, furniture layout, materials, color, and lighting coalesce into a coherent and stimulating whole.

0.1

What does this book propose to do?

—

This book attempts to do two things: to impart knowledge that will prove useful to you as you explore and progress along your journey into design, and to try to share some of the amazing emotions and feelings—the excitement and the enjoyment—of creating environments and realizing spaces where the theater of interior design connects with individuals to make their lives better and more fulfilled. The text explains essential concepts in a logical and sensible way by looking at the process of design, from first contact with a client, to presentation of the finished design work, and beyond. This book introduces each aspect and leaves the way open for further and more advanced study.

It is the emotional, creative aspect of design that often draws people to apprentice themselves to this exciting discipline, and here the images that accompany the text are intended to inspire as well as explain. Looking at the work of established designers is a good way to learn and to open the eyes of a new designer to the possibilities of the discipline that they have undertaken.

Being inspired and passionate about creating are some of the most important aspects of a designer's personality. Design is often defined as an exercise in problem solving, and while it is, this is not the whole story. A passion to make things better, more exciting, and more beautiful is also very much what interior design is about.

In this second edition, we have included additional case studies and interviews at the end of the first seven chapters. We have also introduced activities for students; these exercises will help to reinforce their understanding and further their learning of interior design.

1.1

The Design Process

The "design process" is a term that covers a set of operations which, when carefully undertaken by the designer, result in a thoroughly considered and well-crafted design solution that meets the needs of the client.

Design might be seen as a largely linear activity with a start point (at which the client makes first contact with the designer) and an end point when the project has been implemented. However, the reality is that within the process, many of the individual tasks are interrelated, so changes to one element of a design solution may require that earlier parts of the process are revisited and revised. In this context, process is a means to an end; it isn't always appropriate to be dogmatic about following the process. It provides structure, a framework to follow, but it must remain flexible enough such that insight, research, and developments can all be harnessed as and when they arise to take your ideas onto a new and better level.

You should try to see the design process as a malleable one where the different tasks are adaptable to the unique nature of each project. The design process is not a standard "one size fits all" solution, and you will need to develop your understanding of it so that you can see how it might be used to meet the needs of individual projects that you work on.

One concern that should be addressed at every stage of the design process is that of sustainability, which has become a most important consideration; Chapter 7 discusses this in more detail.

1.1

By following a structured design process and by carefully considering the needs of their client, Project Orange has created a calm and reflective interior for this house in Suffolk, England.

The design process in action

—

In the following description of the major parts of the design process, the comments made earlier about its flexibility should be borne in mind; any or all of the actions described here could be adapted to suit individual projects. It will also become clear that the job of a designer actually involves a great deal of general administration work in addition to the design element of a project. When working as part of a large practice, this may not be especially apparent as job roles will probably be tightly defined. In smaller companies, however, the designer may find themselves deeply involved in all aspects of the process.

Analysis

—

Analysis is relevant at two related, but distinct, parts of the project cycle. In the very earliest stages, before in-depth design work takes place, the designer will need to assess the scale and complexity of the project work to be undertaken. This will allow preliminary estimates to be made of the time and resources needed to complete the project, and these will in turn provide a foundation upon which the designer can base a fee proposal. Part of the work at this stage will involve determining the scope of the project and the likely format and content of the presentation (or early "schematic design"), as this will control, to a large degree, the amount of drawings and visuals that are prepared, all of which take time that will need to be charged to the client.

Following this, and once the client has agreed to the proposed design work being undertaken to reach the first presentation stage, the designer can take an in-depth brief from the client. Initial examination of the brief, allied to a general understanding of the project, will give the designer a starting point for further research. All of this work will lead to the second tranche of analysis, in which the designer is aiming to edit, distill, and ultimately make sense of all the information that has been gathered. Some of the information will relate to the practical aspects of the brief, some to the aesthetic, and some of it could be contradictory in nature. Over time, the designer will become used to setting priorities and reaching a comfortable compromise with regard to conflicting information. It is very rare to find a project that does not need some element of compromise to succeed, but there is never one single way to deal with it. Each project must be looked at on its own merits, and decisions must be reached that reflect the unique nature of the project.

Once analysis is complete, conclusions regarding the style and content of the project can be summarized by creating a concept. This will then be used to generate ideas and drive the project. Different methods of analysis and concept styles are looked at in greater detail in the next chapter, but whatever approach is taken, the concept is key to the success of the project.

1.2

This diagram represents the stages of the design process, though each element may change or be adapted as required by the project; it does not show the relative amount of work required for each task; again, this will vary from project to project.

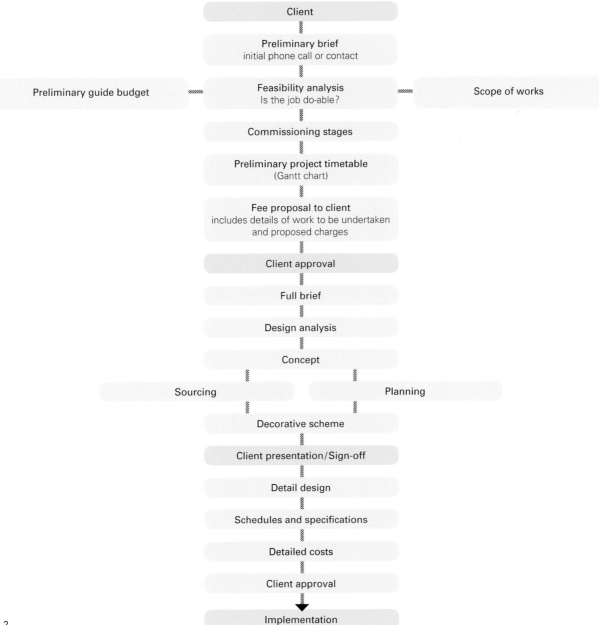

Client

Preliminary brief
initial phone call or contact

Preliminary guide budget — Feasibility analysis
Is the job do-able? — Scope of works

Commissioning stages

Preliminary project timetable
(Gantt chart)

Fee proposal to client
includes details of work to be undertaken
and proposed charges

Client approval

Full brief

Design analysis

Concept

Sourcing — Planning

Decorative scheme

Client presentation/Sign-off

Detail design

Schedules and specifications

Detailed costs

Client approval

Implementation

1.2

13

Development

—

The development stage (or "design development" phase as it's sometimes known) of the project is one of the most interesting for the designer. It is where the natural talents of most designers find their expressive outlet and where the individual can really make a mark on a project. This is the stage where the needs of the client are taken and transformed into a workable, practical, and aesthetic design solution. It is where ideas are generated and given life, where "flights of fancy" are captured and turned into feasible and stunning reality. The discovery of an idea and the realization that it can be used and made into something special is exciting; it is an experience that designers live for. It motivates and helps spur the designer on to discover more of what the project holds. Interior design is problem solving on a large and complex scale, but we are also adding the aesthetic touches, the humanizing elements, that make interiors appealing and functional on an emotional level.

Development work can sometimes be hard, requiring a great deal of thought and reworking until the result is as perfect as is practicable, but the pleasure and pride that the designer experiences when it goes well are worth the effort.

How much development work needs to be undertaken depends very much upon exactly what the client requires from the designer. If the client expects to see "concept sketches" for a project, then only minimal design work may need to be undertaken; just enough basic space planning and the development of a few decorative ideas or motifs, for example, to allow the designer to produce sketch visuals of the proposals. If, however, the client wants to see a fully resolved design solution, then a great deal of development work will be undertaken; space planning, decorative details, and bespoke items will all need to be worked on, and this will generate a much larger number of drawings and supporting work.

During this stage, many different strands of the finished design will be coming together. Space planning will be a major priority. Taking account of ergonomic needs, the designer will seek to create a balanced and effective furniture layout that meets the functional needs of the user. The designer will be sourcing furniture, finishes, and fabrics that will be chosen for their aesthetic and practical fit with the concept, with space-planning constraints also informing furniture choices. As the decorative scheme begins to take shape, the collection of finishes will be refined and edited.

The design is likely to be quite fluid, changing and evolving while heading toward a fully resolved finale. Being open to change is one of the best qualities a designer can have. It is by being open and seeing where the development process leads that unique breakthroughs in the design can be made.

1.3

1.4

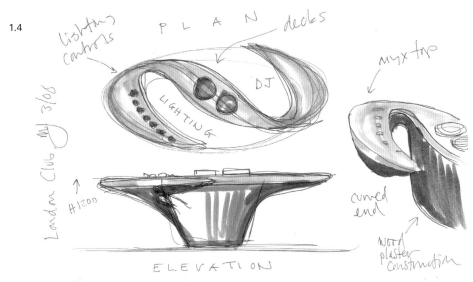

1.3

These are two quick but considered perspective sketches by Mark Humphrey, which have been drawn as part of the design development process in order to help in the visualization of different aspects of an interior.

1.4

This is another sketch by Mark Humphrey, which was created to rationalize his ideas for a DJ booth at a London club. This simple sketch embodies the essence of the concept, and the ideas it shows will be developed further through more sketches and accurate working drawings that will provide a fabricator with the information needed to create the piece for real.

Thinking on paper

—

Whatever form ideas may take, getting them out of your head and onto paper is crucial to being able to see the issues clearly. It is not enough to try to "think things through" and then create a drawing to record a finished idea, as almost no one is gifted enough to be able to foresee a fully resolved and articulated design. Instead, it is through the act of drawing itself that issues are identified and resolved. This is such an important point for the novice designer to grasp: drawings are not made simply to record an idea or detail that has already been formulated in the designer's mind. Instead, making drawings is a process of "thinking on paper." Drawing is crucial to the development of a design, an extremely powerful tool in the designer's arsenal. Sketching and hand drawing play a part in the lives of almost all designers; even those who use computers on a daily basis turn their ideas into the drawings used for construction purposes.

Quick sketches and formal technical drawings are used in conjunction to conceive new ideas and examine their impact on the scheme. Plans are usually the first technical drawings to be made, but as soon as the first planning options are being explored, the designer should be thinking in three dimensions, so elevations, sections, or perspective sketches will follow to show other aspects of the space. Drawing is an excellent way of comparing alternatives, of seeing different options side by side.

After the project has been presented to the client, and the client has approved the work to date, further drawings will be needed to move the project forward. These drawings, done in more detail than those for the presentation, will be sent out to tender to allow accurate quotes to be given by potential contractors.

They will highlight what work needs to be done to the space and, where necessary, will show constructional details, thus ensuring that the designer's vision for the project is realized by the contractors as intended.

It should be said that, while the designer is always aiming to provide the best solution possible, the solution is almost certainly going to include compromises. At the very least, there will be competing, if not conflicting, needs and wants in almost every design brief. It is the job of the designer to make judgments and to prioritize. In some situations, it will be the practical solution that is the most appropriate; in others, the aesthetic will win. You will be able to make these judgments by referring to your design analysis and concept.

Implementation

—

After all the design work has been agreed to and signed off by the client, implementation (or construction administration) can begin. Once contractors have been engaged to carry out the work, the involvement of the designer could be minimal, with a number of site visits to check that work is being accomplished as intended. The designer could, on the other hand, be involved in a very hands-on supervisory role.

In some countries, depending on the depth of training that the designer has undertaken, legislation may limit their involvement with the implementation process. The term "project management" is sometimes restricted to those who have undertaken specific training in that subject, so the designer may find legal limitations on what they are able to contribute to this part of the process.

Even if this is the case, it is likely that the designer's input will be required to resolve some of the issues that are bound to arise as the implementation progresses. A good relationship with contractors and others involved in the project will be a great help, and this can in part be achieved by proving that you understand some of the problems that may arise during the implementation phase. Knowledge of building practice, materials and their limitations, and local building regulations, will all give the designer credibility with those in the building trade. Neat, legible, and complete drawings are vital in communicating with the construction team. As part of the development stage, you will have tried to anticipate all the drawings that will be required for the various trades involved with the project to interpret your instructions accurately. This may well be a much greater number of drawings than was needed to communicate your design proposals to the client. Even at the implementation stage it may be necessary to create new drawings to deal with some of the unexpected and unforeseen situations that arise.

Long-term professional relationships with tradespeople are often forged by designers, with the same contractors being used time and time again for their projects. The trust that is built up in this way can be very helpful to the easy running of the project, allowing for a more efficient workflow because of the familiarity that exists with the designer's ways of working. Good workmen will trust and respect the designer's judgment, even if this means working outside of their experience, but this trust can take time to mature. If contractors are not known to the designer, then it is especially important that the designer maintains a professional attitude at all times. All drawings must be thorough and complete. Decisions made and changes agreed need to be fully documented and recorded, as disagreements could be costly and cause friction between the parties involved.

1.5

1.5

As construction on-site progresses, the implications of design decisions begin to take shape. A new staircase linking two floors requires structural works to an existing floor slab, which the building can accommodate with relative ease. Here, the opening has been created in the slab, which is awaiting the new structural steel to support the staircase. Note that health and safety regulations have been observed with the provision of a temporary barrier.

Evaluation

—

It is healthy for a designer to constantly question the chain of decisions that have been taken to that point and to maintain a self-critical attitude toward everything throughout the life of a project. Before reaching the implementation stage, revising work that has already been done can be a healthy way to work.

From the client's point of view, the design process is usually considered complete after the implementation stage, but the designer should also evaluate the project in an effort to learn from it. A time of reflection will be valuable immediately after the design has been delivered, as lessons learned during the process will still be fresh in the mind, and it is good practice to revisit the project after an appropriate period has elapsed (say six months or a year), as lessons might be learned which become apparent only after a space has been occupied and is functional. While it may or may not be possible to rectify any shortcomings that are identified on an individual project at this stage, the knowledge acquired can be fed into subsequent projects.

Whatever the extent of the work undertaken to try to visualize the finished outcome of the project during the design development, there will be some instances where you can only properly judge some of your aesthetic decisions during implementation. Although it may be possible to make changes at this stage, there are likely to be cost implications. It may be more appropriate to simply learn the lesson for next time but take no action on-site.

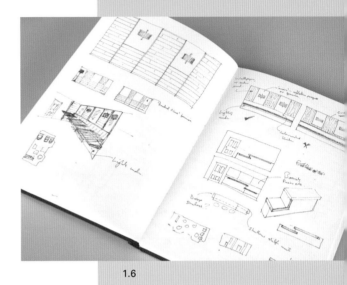

1.6

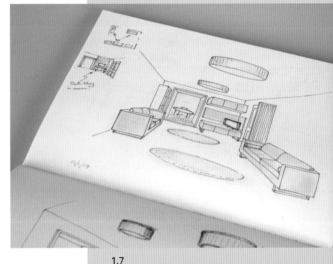

1.7

Thinking point: The importance of drawing

—

Drawing is an activity that you may well not have taken part in for some time before coming to design training. It can, therefore, by very intimidating, but you need to understand that you don't have to be an accomplished artist in order to be a good designer. What you do need is a willingness to commit ideas to paper and to not be afraid of what others might think of your drawing abilities. Experienced designers do not judge the quality of the sketch; they evaluate the idea that the sketch is expressing. Formal, accurate, technical drawings (plans, elevations, and sections, for example) are created on the drawing board or on the computer, and the techniques for producing them are skills that most people can learn. Sketches, on the other hand, are freehand drawings that can be rough, immediate, and expressive, or more carefully executed. However they are arrived at, sketches exist to quickly capture and communicate ideas; they are not necessarily meant to be beautiful representational drawings.

1.6

This sketchbook shows rough ideas that have been captured very quickly. The sketchbook has been used as a notebook, and the ideas shown will be looked at and further developed at a later stage. Most designers will keep at least one sketchbook close to hand almost all the time so that they can easily record ideas as they occur.

1.7

This spontaneous but considered freehand perspective drawing was created in the presence of the client to help expand upon ideas shown in formal presentation drawings. Sketches like these are invaluable for answering questions that clients pose during presentation.

1.8

This is a rendered plan showing a bedroom and bathroom configuration at a hotel in St. Petersburg, Russia. Drawings such as this will help the designer to develop the concept into a workable design solution and will form the basis of the presentation to the client, but many more drawings will have to be made to enable the implementation of the design.

1.8

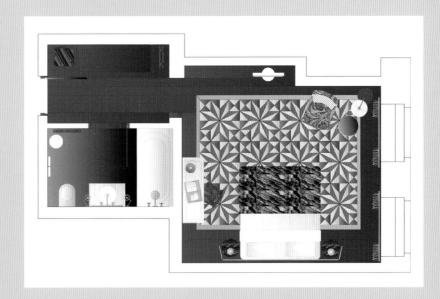

Professional practice

—

"Professional practice" is a term that covers the personal qualities and business procedures of the designer, and also the framework of regulation that the designer is subject to while working. The latter falls outside the scope of this book, as the laws that govern design work vary considerably from country to country, and they are frequently subject to change. Some basic and universal business practices are, however, worth looking at.

What makes a good designer?

—

Designers are creative people, and being organized does not always come naturally to a creative personality. It is, however, a trait that all designers would do well to cultivate, as there is so much more to the business of design than just designing. Being organized is probably the most important facet of a professional attitude. For those who get involved in the full range of tasks associated with the day-to-day operation of a design practice, it could be that they will spend no more than 20% of their time actively pursuing the development of a design. The other 80% can easily be taken up by the more mundane side of running a business: administration, filing, emailing, traveling, and so on.

Allied to good organization skills are good time management skills. Interior design is a subject that it is easy to be passionate about, meaning it is easy to spend a disproportionate amount of time on the design work, to the detriment of other tasks that need to be undertaken if a project is to be completed successfully. To help with this, one of the first things to be done on a project is to create a project plan that shows the tasks that need to be addressed in order to successfully complete the project. Probably the most useful way of visualizing the project plan is in the form of a Gantt chart: a horizontal bar chart that illustrates a project schedule. Strictly speaking, a true Gantt chart shows the outcomes of a project and not the actions that will be undertaken to reach those outcomes, but for most designers this distinction is academic and can be ignored. Software, including free open-source programs, is available to help produce project schedules.

Attention to detail is a typical character trait of a designer. This may well be in evidence through the design development phase, but it is also important at the very end of a project when the minor imperfections and errors in the scheme as implemented need to be identified and corrected by the contractors. This process is the final opportunity for the designer to make sure that the project is resolved satisfactorily.

How much should you charge?

—

How designers should charge for their services is one of the questions that new designers are usually anxious about. Over time, three main models for charging (with many variations on them) have appeared and can be summarized as:

→ Charging a percentage of the overall project value.

→ Charging only for items supplied by the designer (such as furniture) with a markup fee.

→ Charging a design fee based on an assessment or projection of hours worked on the project.

Arguably, the most appropriate method of charging is to agree on a design fee. This means that the client can see what is being paid for directly, without fees being "hidden" in other charges, as is the case when a markup is added to goods supplied. It also means that payment is made within a reasonable amount of time of the work being done, and that financial commitments on the client are kept to a minimum as charges for each stage of the project are agreed before work is undertaken. However the designer decides to charge, an open and transparent system will be to the benefit of all.

While it is helpful that the relationship between designer and client is a friendly one, it is still vital to have a written contract or formal agreement between both parties for their legal protection. This will define the type of services provided and their scope, the fee structure, dispute resolution, copyright issues, and what is expected of both designer and client. Trade associations in many countries will

have standard documents that can be used in these cases, but even if this is not so, contracts can be drawn up with the assistance of a legal professional, which will protect the interests of all concerned.

Designers should realize that they are not alone when undertaking a project. Other professionals can be brought in as required to add their expertise to the project. Structural engineers, surveyors, quantity surveyors, and project managers are examples, and they all play their part in making the project happen with delivery to the client as close to being on time and on budget as possible.

1.9

This project timetable is presented in the form of a Gantt chart and shows the key stages of a project. These charts are a very useful way of showing the tasks or stages involved in a project.

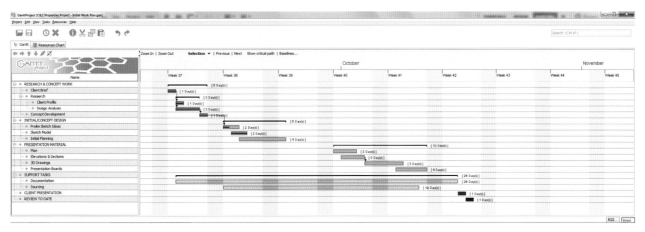

1.9

Case study: Small Batch Coffee Company, UK

The Small Batch Coffee Company was established in 2007 in Brighton, a cosmopolitan city on the south coast of England with a strong creative and media sector. The company wanted to develop an authentic coffee experience with a sense of place, which was different to the large multinational brands such as Starbucks and Costa Coffee.

Chalk Architecture was the firm responsible for the interior design of the Small Batch outlets. They not only designed the new premises, but they were also involved in developing the identity for the Small Batch brand. The identity consisted of logos, which evolved during the design process and were integrated into the interior design of the various coffee shops. These included motifs, such as the "dome," which they were able to incorporate into the interior design and can be used in a variety of situations and combinations.

Small Batch wanted their brand identity to be playful and in tune with its range of customers and also to be flexible, so that it could be adapted to meet the requirements of the different site locations. For example, in a city center unit, the logo is stripped back and appears in unexpected places such as on the base of the stools, and in another location it appears as a stencil graffitied outside the premises. In this way, the identity can be placed into the interior in a variety of subtle ways, which creates a more personal and site-specific dimension, which is quite different to the more uniform approach to interior design of many larger, more global brands.

1.10

1.10

This Small Batch outlet is located in a busy street in Brighton, UK. The front of the building is decorated with gold domes and playful graffiti.

The pace of opening of the outlets allowed for a variety of different responses to be created; in an urban situation it had to catch the eye of a fast-moving, high footfall of shoppers outside and encourage them into the outlet. Table and chair settings became high stools and high tables, elevating people's eyeline to a normal state relative to the street. The raised seating plan also made the space feel like it had more bustle, as customers sit shoulder to shoulder when it's busy, and it allows them to comfortably watch the world go by outside. These agile design responses create solutions of local relevance rather than the more uniform "one size fits all" approach of the larger international brands in the marketplace.

One of the interesting aspects that the designers at Chalk Architecture bring to the process is their upcycling and reuse of materials from one project to another. They might rip something out of one site, an old house for example, and use it in a different project. This provides a cross-pollination of materials throughout their work.

1.11

1.12

1.11

The flexible logo sometimes appears in unexpected places like the dome brand burnt into the base of the stool.

1.12

Response to the site is important, here the high stools increase customer visibility and create strong graphic lines.

Interview: **Chalk Architecture**

Paul Nicholson is the director and founder of Chalk Architecture based in Brighton, UK. He worked closely with Small Batch to develop their identity.

You developed the Small Batch identity right from the start. What provided your inspiration? Did the client have a clear idea of what he wanted and was he involved in the process?

→ It's all about the coffee, whether it be sourcing, trading, transporting, roasting, supplying, blending, filtering, selling, buying, or enjoying. The Small Batch experience touches each of these activities one way or another depending on which site you visit. We were clear from the start that the design of the branding and the interior needed to evoke a sense of the story of coffee. The level of attention to detail underpins the Small Batch concept; it is driven by their business ethic and reflected in all aspects of their environment and service.

There are many coffee shop brands both locally and internationally. How did you identify a gap in the market where you could grow?

→ One of the things that we identified is that Brighton consists of identifiable micro-village zones. In developing the brand, we recognized that each of these sites required a unique response, which is reflected in the design of each unit.

1.13

How did you develop the design and concept? What methods did you use to develop the concept and communicate your ideas to the client?

→ We still work in a traditional way of presenting colored plans, elevations, and sketch visuals. The materials are the key, and working up detailed maquettes with the fit-out contractor is a critical part of the process.

You have developed a strategy that creates a unique atmosphere for each Small Batch outlet. How do you develop these individual identities?

→ We are always exploring sources of reclaimed materials, and these relationships take time to develop. The identity of each new store depends in part on which materials we have available at the time.

1.13

There is a focus, where possible, on sourcing reclaimed materials; this works with the brand's ethos and also helps to keep the costs low.

Activity

—

01. Think about the interactions that a designer may have with other professions.

→ Which professions may be part of the design process?

→ Which professions may be part of the regulatory process?

→ At what stage of the design process is it appropriate or beneficial for the interior designer to engage with the other professions that you have identified?

02. As the designer works through the different stages of the design process, there is a need to balance many conflicting demands in order to create a successful design solution.

Much of this is a consideration of the practical versus the aesthetic. This is not to say that a practical interior cannot look good (and vice versa), but there is often a clear tension between these two demands.

→ Select five iconic interior spaces. Ideally, some should be ones that you can visit, but failing that, choose spaces that you can experience through multiple images and written descriptions, and decide where in these spaces the balance lies between the practical and the aesthetic.

→ Is there a clear divide?

→ Do you believe the designer's choices were successful?

→ Justify your answers.

Understanding the Project

The first stages of a project are the foundation on which the whole design process will either stand or fall; investing adequate time at this stage is crucial if the project is to have a good chance of success. Spending time to make sure that each aspect of the project is clearly identified will deepen your understanding of the task ahead, and it will open up new avenues for exploration as the design evolves.

Teasing out information from a brief can be a long process and isn't always fulfilling in itself, but it allows you to research and formulate a concept; and strong concepts (key ideas) are what the most successful projects have at their heart.

There are several steps to achieving your goal of understanding the project, from meeting the client and taking a brief from them, to developing a concept. Each step is looked at in more detail in this chapter.

2.1

2.1

BDP were asked to design a retail outlet for Fritz Hansen. The staircase became the focal point of the design where the clean lines and restrained palette of the interior are realized.

The client

—

Clients can be anyone from anywhere. A client might just as easily be a company, an organization, or an individual. However, as clients, they all have a common need for the services of an interior designer, though the level of understanding of these needs is likely to vary greatly between them.

For some, the decision to engage a professional designer will have been arrived at after a careful appraisal of their circumstances. For others, it will be a vague idea that there is likely to be someone (the designer) who can provide better answers to their problem than they would be able to arrive at themselves. Some clients may believe that aesthetics are the main issue, and the practical side of their needs may not have featured in their decision to call in the designer at all. For others, practicalities may be the prime consideration, with decorative concerns a secondary issue.

It is for these reasons, and many others, that the designer needs to be able to communicate on many levels with lots of different personality types. From the forthright to the timid, clients need to be understood, treated with respect, and made to understand that they are a key element of the design process.

Because you will often be trying to connect with a client on an emotional level, establishing a good rapport is a must. In fact, it is sometimes a more important part of building a good client/designer relationship than being able to provide an extensive curriculum vitae.

Client profile

—

The client profile is an attempt to understand better who the client is and how they live or work. It is a general overview and while in itself it may not relate directly to the brief that the client has given, it will provide insights that will help you as you develop your design.

In a residential project, the client profile can help you to understand how the space might be used on a daily basis from first thing in the morning until last thing at night, and it may also give some clues as to style preferences of the client. An understanding of the daily routine can be one of the most vital parts of producing a design that works for the client.

For commercial projects, understanding the work practices of the organization that will ultimately occupy the space is essential. This is another opportunity to look closely at the status quo and determine if the existing work patterns make best use of the space. You may find that they do, or you may be able to challenge these and propose new and better ways of working. Commercial clients often employ designers not just to create comfortable working environments, but as "agents of change" when they know that a new direction will benefit their organization.

Case study: **The client brief**

Finn Erikson runs a product design consultancy called Finn Design in Brighton on the south coast of England. The location is in a bohemian area full of creative companies.

Finn Design has clients ranging from Muji and Apple, to Bang & Olufsen, who visit frequently. He employs between eight and twelve staff. Most staff have their own desks, but some work in shared areas.

The space must reflect his philosophy: "We care about our designs and our designers." These values are popular with his clients as the studio produces excellent designs, and they are happy that he cares for his staff.

Finn is moving to a three-story building with a spacious warehouse feel. The move should develop his identity and provide more extensive facilities for his staff and his clients.

Finn is looking for design solutions that provide:

→ A clear expression of his philosophy

→ Creative and imaginative use of space that will reflect and enhance his business

→ Integration of spaces and finishes that maintain the feel of the existing warehouse space

→ A considered material and color palette that is both inspiring and practical

The following areas need to be provided:

Welcome area: this is where clients gain their first impressions of the organization, so it is important that it provides the correct ambience and allows the guests to be greeted in an appropriate manner.

Studio: this requires fixed work units for a minimum of eight designers. Each will have a computer and storage space, as well as a small work area and pinup wall space. The designers need to be arranged in groups in a studio environment, which should have a creative feel and have some privacy screening. All workspaces must conform to the relevant ergonomic regulations and guidelines.

Meeting rooms: one area is to be used as a presentation room for up to twelve people; this requires some acoustic privacy and the ability to control lighting levels. In addition, there should be at least two other meeting spaces for more casual use by smaller groups.

Work area for Finn: he likes to be "hands on" and he is frequently in development meetings with his teams. He also needs his own quiet space in order to think and liaise with clients and suppliers.

Display and resources area: this space is the heart of the studio. It needs to be interactive and have a sourcing area, as well storage for materials, product information, and prototypes.

Social space and beverage area: this is where staff can relax, have informal meetings, and make drinks.

Washrooms: these should be spacious and private; have the usual facilities, plus a shower room and lockers; and have a high level of finish to reflect the company's designs.

The brief

—

The briefing from the client is the first real chance that you will have to get a feel for a project. Some clients present their briefs as carefully constructed documents that fully convey the scope and detail of the project; other briefs may be little more than a casual chat over a cup of coffee.

Although a written brief is likely to contain a good deal of useful information, quantity by itself does not necessarily mean quality. In 1657, French mathematician, physicist, and philosopher Blaise Pascal wrote, "I have made this letter longer than usual, only because I have not had the time to make it shorter." Information that is succinct and relevant is the essence of a successful briefing document. In fact, brevity is often a good thing. If the brief is focused and clear, it will be easier for the designer to make incisive decisions and to formulate an effective design solution.

Understanding the brief

—

It is quite reasonable to ask the client to produce a written brief after their initial contact with you, and prior to the briefing meeting. This is a good tactic because it will force the client to carefully consider their request, and it will also make sure that they are serious about the idea of engaging an interior designer. The chance to talk about the written brief at a later date will allow both parties to sort out any problems or uncertainties that arise from it. The opportunity for mutual agreement is one that should be made the most of; time spent talking over the brief will give both sides a better understanding of each other's position and can only have a positive effect on the business relationship.

The more complete the brief, the easier your job should be. However, you must remember that you may be dealing with amorphous feelings and ideas about the desired end point of a project, rather than a definitive list of needs. It is entirely possible that the "brief" may consist of the client saying no more than, "I just want somewhere that's a great place to come back to after a hard day's work."

Some clients include practical issues that need to be addressed in the brief. Others may talk in general, abstract terms about the emotional response that they want their space to trigger.

Are there any constraints?

Even if the brief is vague, there may be some constraints that you can establish: time, budget, style, and so on. The word "constraint" sounds negative, but you should actively be trying to seek out the constraints present in the brief. Constraints are actually good; you should look at them as a positive force within the design analysis that will help you define the scope of the project. When a brief seems complex or daunting, the natural constraints can be some of the first elements that help you see the shape of the project.

Many projects, whether domestic or commercial, will have more than one individual as the client. You should try to make sure that, whoever has written the brief or whoever you have spoken to in your meetings, the final brief has been agreed to by everyone who has a stake in the finished project. You also need to take the opportunity at face-to-face meetings to be certain that you and the client understand each other explicitly; what does the client think of when they say "contemporary"? Is their understanding of the word the same as yours? This is the time to find out.

2.2

2.2

The island in this modern kitchen has been designed to blend in well with the rest of the kitchen area and to provide a number of useful functions. The countertop matches the floor. Extra kitchen storage is supplied by the cupboards at either end of the island, and there is seating and dining space for the family.

Design analysis

—

Having met the client and taken a brief, the detailed analysis can begin. You need to be sure that you understand all that the client needs. Sometimes this will have been explicitly stated, at other times you will have to make inferences from the information that you have.

You will need to perform a careful balancing act with the raw information. Your judgment will be crucial in deciding whether the client has actually understood their own needs. Remember that clients have engaged you because they believe that they need a professional, which implies that they are not experts, so some of the assumptions they have made may not be correct, and it will be down to you to put them right.

2.3

New ideas, new solutions

—

If you were to produce a finished design solution where you had managed to "tick all the boxes," a client ought to be content with the solution provided. But "content" is not what you should be aiming for. Something extraordinary, even revolutionary, can often only be realized when you don't simply provide the client with the answer that they think they need. Special things happen when insight leads to turning an idea on its head, or doing something contrary to what the client is expecting, or doing it in a way that hasn't been done before—a way that will answer the brief in a better, more efficient, or more beautiful way. Unusual ideas will need to be thoroughly tested and resolved during the later development stages of the design process to ensure that they really do work, but it is these ideas that will yield a delighted client, not just one who is content.

2.3

This composite image has been produced during research into the site. It consists of several prints that have been roughly collaged together, and as a unique visual reference, it provides an evocative sense of the location of the project. Although technology might be thought to have made this "hand-crafted" approach to visual research obsolete, it should be noted that using such craft-based techniques to recording your research provides a useful opportunity for contemplation, which can be very helpful.

Thinking point: Question the brief

—

What is arguably one of the most iconic buildings in the world owes its form and success to an architect who didn't hesitate to question the brief. The building is Fallingwater by Frank Lloyd Wright in Mill Run, Pennsylvania, USA.

The client, Edgar J. Kaufmann, took Wright to his site on Bear Run where he wanted to build a summer house. With broadleaf trees and rhododendron bushes all around, the site overlooked the river at a point where it cascades over a waterfall. At the same time, Kaufmann also gave Wright a survey of the site, which he had commissioned some time earlier. This site survey drawing showed the river toward the northern part of the site, the waterfall, and the hillside to the south of the waterfall. It was clear from the way that the site plan had been laid out that Kaufmann expected to build his house on the hillside south of the river. From this situation, there would be a view of the waterfall to the north.

However, Wright wasn't content with this interpretation of the landscape. Instead, without any consultation with the client and using the new technology of reinforced concrete, he proposed a design for the house that integrated it completely into the site by using a cantilever construction to launch the house out over the river, above the waterfall, from the northern hillside. Wright said to Kaufmann, "I want you to live with the waterfall, not just look at it, but for it to become an integral part of your lives." In so doing, he created the building for which he is probably best known, and he gave his client an experience of, and an involvement with, the site far beyond what was originally anticipated.

2.4

2.4

For one of his most iconic buildings—Fallingwater in Pennsylvania, USA—Frank Lloyd Wright proposed a design that boldly questioned his client's brief. Rather than situate the house away from the waterfall, he decided to integrate it completely into the site.

Analyzing information

—

You may imagine that "analysis" means an intellectual and academic dissection of the data from the brief. This is a factor of most analyses, but it can be a visual exercise as well as a literary one. You are, after all, going to be exploring the aesthetic side of the brief in addition to the practical. You will also be working visually with media such as collage, sketching, and photography, which will help you form links and develop aesthetic ideas in a free and potentially unrestricted way. This style of working is a fast and efficient way for a creative mind to access new ideas as they emerge from the brief, and it connects well with the building and site research that will be looked at later. Ultimately, if you are to produce an effective analysis, you should feel able to work in any way or medium that makes you feel comfortable. This is a skill that may need practice, but it is also a rewarding one that pays dividends.

Two well-recognized techniques that can help in the process of analysis and evaluation are brainstorming and mindmapping. Brainstorming is an activity designed to generate a large number of ideas; it is usually undertaken as a group activity, but there is no reason why the principles should not be applied to solo sessions. Four basic rules underpin the process:

→ The quantity of ideas is important; more ideas equate to a greater chance of finding an effective solution.

→ Ideas are not criticized, at least not in the early stages of the exercise—that can come later when all the ideas have been generated. Ideas that might have some drawbacks could be built on to produce stronger ideas.

→ Unusual, offbeat ideas are encouraged. They may suggest radical new ways of solving a problem.

→ Ideas can be combined to produce better solutions.

Mind maps are diagrams that are used to visually represent ideas and associations surrounding a central thought or problem. There is no formal method for organizing the map. Instead, it grows organically and allows the designer to arrange and link the information in any way that feels right, though the different points are naturally organized into groups or areas. Pictures, doodles, and color are as much a part of a mind map as are words; imagery helps to reinforce ideas and the visual pattern created is easier for the brain to process and contemplate than a simple list, encouraging subconscious processing of the information at some later point.

Once you are satisfied that you have extracted as much information from the brief as you can, you will have a secure foundation upon which to build your project research, which is detailed in the following sections.

35

2.5

This mind map was created for a refurbishment project. As a method of organizing ideas and information, the visual and nonlinear format helps in the generation of new ideas and enables connections to be more easily seen.

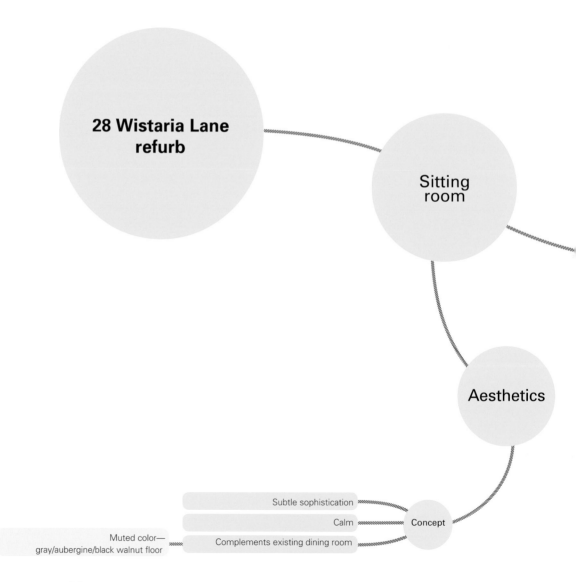

28 Wistaria Lane refurb

Sitting room

Aesthetics

Subtle sophistication

Calm

Muted color—gray/aubergine/black walnut floor

Complements existing dining room

Concept

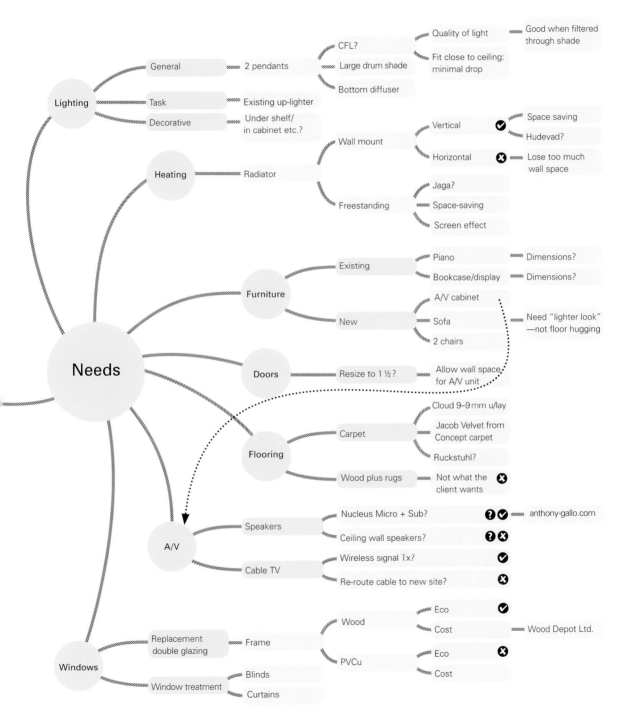

Design research

—

No design for a space should ignore the existing building into which it is being integrated. An understanding of what exists is fundamental to deciding what needs to be done if the space is to accommodate the functions that will take place there.

Broadly speaking, research may be of one of two forms: "soft" or "hard." Hard research deals with facts and figures, numbers, details of the building that can be classified and measured (for example, a measured survey), and soft research is about feelings, inferences, and intuition—our emotional response to a space. Both are valid types of research to use when trying to understand a space, though they may be recorded and used in very different ways.

When you are creating interiors within newly built structures, there will be a lot of scope to define the look and feel of the interior. However, where the interior is placed within an existing building, the designer is obliged to understand how the previous life of the building has given the space its character. This feeling of character or history, the spirit of a place (its genius loci), is strengthened by the proportions of the volume and the position of existing building elements, such as windows and doorways, all of which will impose a certain sense of order upon the space. The new design can respond to these factors, allowing them to inform the new design. The appreciation of a building's history may extend beyond the boundaries of the property to include the local area, the street, the village, and the city where it stands.

None of this means that your design should be a pastiche of the existing style references of the building. The best designs respect the existing building and will reference it in some way in their execution—through materials, methods of construction, craftsmanship, pattern, form, and so on—but may be of a radically different style to that which already exists.

All of the preceding research should bring you to a position where you understand the essential points that will have an impact on the design:

→ What structure exists? What are its materials? How is it oriented?

→ What functions and activities will take place? How will these be addressed practically? What furniture is required, for example?

→ What is possible in the space (and just as importantly, what is not possible, due to time, technical, or budget limitations)?

→ How does the space function and interact with others around it?

→ What emotional response does the client want the space to generate in the user? What aesthetic style is desired?

This is necessary, but for the design to feel considered and complete, rather than being a random collection of elements, there is a need to find a unifying idea that will hold the disparate parts of the design together. This single idea will be one that sets the stylistic tone of the design. It is this single idea that is the concept.

2.6

Case study: **Researching the existing site**

Brinkworth, a London-based design agency, was commissioned by artist Dinos Chapman to transform an ordinary Georgian terraced house in London, UK, into an open and flowing family residence. Through an investigation of the site and the building structure, Brinkworth were able to free the internal layout by removing internal walls, and they also extended the space into the garden to create a more interesting relationship between the house and its surroundings.

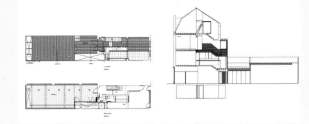

2.8

2.7

2.6

The redesign of the kitchen and staircase enabled the spaces to interact with the rest of the site in a completely new way.

2.7

The more effective use of the available site area allowed for a garden room to be created at the rear of the house.

2.8

The layout plans and section show how the house has been both refigured and extended to create an increased use of the site area.

Researching concepts

—

Concepts can take many forms. They may be visual or literary, found or created. A concept can be embodied in a story, a photo torn from a newspaper, a collage of images, a poem, a pattern on a fragment of used wrapping paper, a page from a scrapbook, or anything that grabs your imagination and provides an anchor. It is a strong and compelling idea that says everything you need about the project: what it looks like, how it feels—the story that it evokes.

However they are presented, the strongest concepts often make little direct reference to the constituent parts of the project. Rather, they are an abstract representation of the ideas of form, texture, color, style, and mood expressed in the brief by the client.

Concepts work by providing a reference point for the designer. All the decisions made during the development of the design, which define the look or feel of the space, can be checked against the concept. Does the formal, grid-like furniture layout you are contemplating work with the concept? Which furniture fabric strengthens the ideas of sophistication and elegance that the client wants? Check against the concept, and you will have your answer.

Communicating concepts

—

Some designers like to work in a very abstract way during the first stages of a project, allowing ideas to coalesce about a central idea. Their concept work could be generated in the form of "mood boards" (or "concept boards"). Others will have strong ideas from the start, and without getting into detailed planning they may confidently produce "concept sketches" that are not intended to be definitive, but which serve to illustrate their first thoughts on how a space might work.

Clients may want to see initial concept work so that they are confident that the design will progress in a direction that they are comfortable with. However, both mood boards and sketches may be very raw, visceral, and unfinished. This is exciting and liberating for the designer, but it can be confusing for the client. You will need to judge the personality of the client and, if necessary, modify the work before presenting it. Careful line drawings organized into an understandable if tentative and unfinished—representation of the space, perhaps with color added to define form, can be a very evocative and ultimately persuasive tool for the designer. Concept work is not about perfection; it is about capturing and communicating the spirit and character of a space.

2.9

2.9

Scrapbooks are a very useful way of collating
research material, especially when this is visual
in nature. Rough working like this encourages
freethinking and helps in the generation of design
ideas during the later stages of the project.

Concept development

—

Project Orange responded at short notice to a brief for the "Urban Interventions" exhibition (part of the London Architecture Biennale) to look at how architecture can reinvent and enhance the fabric of the city. Local architectural practices were asked to submit pieces of work, which were then displayed as a "collection of road signs and street furniture." Housed in a disused 1950s shed, the space was painted yellow in order to lead visitors in from the street, the idea being that they create their own "road map" of the exhibition.

2.10

The yellow of the scheme is the same as that used in road markings outside the venue, and graphics for the exhibition reflect graphics found on road signs, continuing the link.

2.11

The "bar code" floor pattern, derived from the bar code of the Biennale, makes a visual connection between the Biennale and the exhibition as it leads visitors in from the street (at left and right of floor plan).

2.10

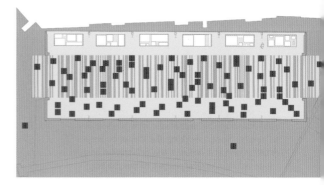

2.11

Thinking point: Visual concepts

—

It is possible to create a visual concept by process rather than by inspiration. This can be helpful when you are under the pressure of deadlines. The technique is to select two or three adjectives from the brief that summarize the experience the client wants from the space. This may be easier than you imagine; clients will often use words such as "sanctuary," "warmth," "urban," "natural," and the like when referring to the feelings they want your finished design to generate, particularly when dealing with a residential project. You can search for images that are strongly suggestive of these adjectives, and create a single unified collage. Generally, you will collect many images and edit them down to those that best illustrate the key adjectives you have chosen (the best imagery to use will be abstract rather than literal, as abstract imagery creates strong but flexible visual concepts; literal images stop the imagination from working and may produce weaker concepts).

Finally, these few images will be further edited to produce a collage in which each image tells its own story and melds with the others to create a single composition, thus reflecting the story that the client wants the space to tell.

Once you have created the concept, the images can be read to give direction for the decorative scheme. Texture, color, form, and style from the concept can all be echoed in the finishes you select, imbuing the completed scheme with the same sensory experience as the concept.

2.12

2.12

This concept collage is exploring the interplay of materials; it was used to examine the texture and colors that might be used in a smart and sophisticated boutique hotel. See the case study on page 44 to find out how these ideas were developed further.

Case study: **Presenting ideas**

For her final major project while studying for her BA (Hons) degree at Portsmouth University, UK, student Hanna Paterson developed proposals for a boutique hotel in central London. The main concept focused around the idea of international business travelers being able to feel relaxed and refreshed after a long journey.

The concept, titled "Static House," is described as follows: "Static House is a concept hotel designed to help global commuters sync their sleep schedules with a desired time zone and reduce the side effects of jet lag. Static introduces a routine throughout the guest's stay, while considering other factors such as temperature, sound, and light to enforce the transition. The concept behind the design is influenced by the levels of sleep and the threshold between reality and dream states in an aim to complement the guest's journey, allowing them to feel a sense of release from any stress. The space is divided up into a series of stages, in order to prepare the individual for sleep."

This was investigated through the ideas of journey, control, observation, scenery, space, and astronomy. The initial ideas were captured through an artifact consisting of a series of photo images, which sought to represent the relationship between the various spaces as planets. This was used to develop and communicate some of Hanna's ideas and the relationship between destination, route, journey, and time, graphically influenced by the idea of constellations.

Hanna had very strong ideas about how the concept could be visualized, and these were developed in a series of models that further explored the ideas from her original artifact. This began to provide some insights into how design could be used to enforce the function of the hotel, and how it could be combined and ordered to create a narrative for her scheme. These initial studies also begin to show how her ideas could be articulated and represented in a three-dimensional way.

After experimenting and researching further into the subject of sleep, travel, and dreams, Hanna chose to define a series of key elements as follows:

→ Route: To enforce guidance

→ Levels: To define the stages

→ Visual: To escape reality and encourage curiosity

→ Landscape: Realistic landscape with unusual twists to create the dreamscape

→ Sensory: Light, sound, and touch

Simple yet playful illustrations were graphically produced alongside the models to reinforce and help visually explain the concept of combining the visualization of the dreamscape and the physical levels and route. These in turn informed the ideas about materials and space for the scheme. In particular, the drawings explore how the ideas of movement and journey may develop around the key themes and how this might integrate within the existing building.

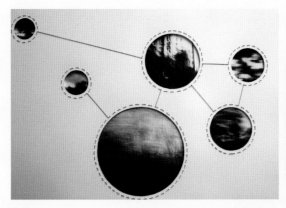

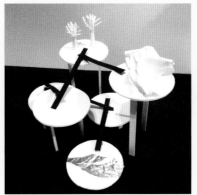

2.13

2.14

2.13

This artifact uses photography and craft elements to form a conceptual map of Hanna's principal ideas.

2.14

Hanna used simple models to illustrate her ideas and the relationships that might develop between the ideas of landscape, space, time, and journey.

2.15

This abstract drawing is one of several that were used to develop Hanna's design ideas and to communicate them in a clear and engaging way.

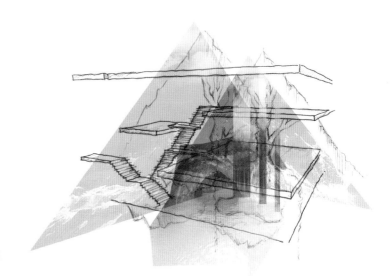

2.15

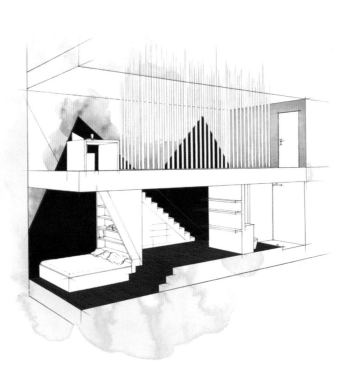

2.16

2.17

2.16

This drawing explores the ideas of journey
and scale within the existing spaces.

2.17

The use of models can help you to express your
ideas clearly to both the design team and the client.
Models also help you to test the design to ensure
that it will work properly and fulfill the brief.

Developing ideas

A monochrome materials palette was used throughout the building, acting as a blank canvas for guests to create their own color experience and light intensity. This not only makes the experience more personal and adaptable but also enables the guests to alter the time of day in a space, reinforcing the aim of syncing their body clock to a suited time zone.

The black-stained timber floor acts as a guide throughout the building, and the raw exposed walls of brick and gray plaster create an unfinished appearance among the clean abstract lines of the installations and the solid black floor, subtly reflecting the idea of the transition between dreamscapes being seamless, unfinished, and ongoing.

Having established and tested her concept, these ideas were then applied more literally by developing the design within the existing building. A variety of methods were used here, including ideas of flow, scale, and journey, to test and establish the validity of Hanna's ideas within the spatial framework.

The final stages tested the design in a more rigorous manner using technical drawings to establish the size, scale, and relationship between the designed spaces through the use of scale drawings, which were produced in plan and section. These drawings help the designer to create and test the spaces as they will be inhabited and are essential for a clear representation of the design as it will be perceived by the prospective user.

This process illustrates how the development of a series of complex ideas can be visualized using a range of simple techniques, which help bring the scheme to life, as well as serving as a useful design tool. It is not necessary to produce realistic drawings to be a designer; however, drawing is a powerful tool that allows ideas to be communicated and represented in a variety of ways. As demonstrated in the previous case study, design is a developing and interactive activity that requires intellectual engagement as well as artistic and visual training.

Case study: **Republic of Fritz Hansen, UK**

Fritz Hansen, a Scandinavian furniture retailer, commissioned Europe's largest design agency, BDP, to create their new Republic of Fritz Hansen showroom. The site was an existing building, comprising 600 square meters (6,458 square feet) of office space over two floors, forming part of an imposing art deco style building in Fitzrovia in London's West End. The selection of the site was important in terms of visibility and footfall but also proximity to clients and the architecture and design community. The site had been used by a media production company and was a tired space, which had been subdivided into a series of smaller spaces.

The Republic's showrooms showcase their furniture—a range of beautiful Scandinavian designs—creating a perfect mix of accessories, furniture, and products to combine retail, showroom, and workspace.

The client's brief was to create a gallery aesthetic to enhance and showcase their products in an appropriate environment with the following spaces:

→ Retail and showroom areas

→ Sales area

→ Workspace for staff

→ Open kitchen

→ Staff washrooms and shower room

→ Storage

One of the early design decisions was to unite the two floors, which were separated, with a staircase and opening that would encourage visitors to flow naturally between the two levels. As the building had a 4.5 meters (approximately 14 feet) grid concrete frame with nonstructural floors, this was relatively easy. However, many configurations of staircase were tested to ensure that it provided a memorable experience through the space.

2.18

The choice of materials provided a simple and honest palette with the extensive use of warm gray screed, oak, and Poul Kjærholm slate on the external steps. The custom-designed staircase incorporates enamelled steel, glass, and oak, which creates an industrial, crafted element reminiscent of Arne Jacobsen. The Fritz Hansen DNA speaks through other elements, such as the burnished oak of the kitchen with its grand-scale high table.

A fully functioning kitchen was designed within the main space; this not only creates a focal point—it also communicates the openness and welcoming nature of Danish culture. This is also reflected in the attention to detail in areas, such as the lighting, which encourages customers to come inside and engages people at night.

The flexibility of the space has allowed areas such as the "experience corner" to be created, which was developed to enhance the customer relationships through the showroom. Here, Fritz Hansen have created an experience similar to buying a car—customers are able to appreciate the materials and get excited about the products, and it allows them to get closer to private customers.

The feedback about the space has been positive. In particular, the flexibility of the space has allowed a wide range of events to take place, for example, events featuring Paul Smith, the fashion designer; Jamie Oliver, the chef and presenter; and the London Philharmonic Orchestra. This means that people from other industries are allowed to use the space, and this helps to broaden the brand's appeal.

2.19

2.18

The staircase was a major focus of the overall design, and the limited material palette created a strong sophisticated scheme.

2.19

The kitchen provides a social focus to the space and continues the restrained palette.

Interview: Fritz Hansen

Jan Vejsholt was the vice president of sales for the UK, Ireland, Middle East, and South Europe for Fritz Hansen. He worked closely with BDP.

Finding an appropriate building was challenging. How important is the building and position in retail design?

→ In terms of location, the footfall was really important as we were moving more toward retail rather than a showroom. Visibility is critical in retail design, and we wanted a prominent ground floor—ideally with a visible lower floor. The split of space was important to us as this provided a balance of the rent, which helped the viability of the project.

Visibility and the relationship with the streetscape are important factors in the design. How do you think that the design exploits the opportunities of the building and communicates the spirit of Fritz Hansen in London?

→ It was important that the language of the building had a fit with the brand and our products, and also an architectural narrative. It is not just the space but the overall language of the building such that "people know that they have arrived at Fritz Hansen."

The designer (Stephen Anderson) worked very closely with us and made us look at the building in a different light; designers are able to look at the space and see the possibilities more objectively.

At the briefing stage there were some specific design elements that were important. Do you feel these were developed and improved through the design process?

→ Our main brief to the designers was to create an open and visible space, which was unfussy, in order that our furniture could speak to our customers. The honesty of our brand is also expressed through decisions such as exposing the services rather than trying to cover them up. Don't hide; incorporate.

The staircase is another iconic element, and we worked closely with the designers to create a journey through the space to entice people downstairs while encouraging them to experience different views through the space and the streetscape outside. We had a strong idea of what we wanted for our identity, and the designers worked with us to create something more than we expected.

How involved were you with the design process and is it important as a client to be informed at all stages, particularly with regards to budget and program?

→ We were new to commercial projects, but the team of designer, project manager, and contractor worked together and really helped navigate us through the process. They preempted pretty much all of the problems before they arrived so that nothing came as a surprise. Overall, the process was a pleasurable experience, and we got exactly what we expected.

2.20

2.20

The overall space creates an open
and flexible retail environment.

Activity

—

01. Think about a building or a space that has made an impression on you. Consider how "hard" research could be used to define some of the physical properties of the space, and then consider how "soft" research could be used to capture your own response, or the responses of others, to the space.

→ What hard research could you undertake into the history and physical properties of the building or space? How would you record it?

→ What soft research could you undertake into your experience of the building/space? What media could you use to record this?

02. How do you anticipate this research informing your design response to a brief?

→ Think about the initial conversations you might have with a client regarding their project.

→ If the project is a residential one, what aspects of the client's lifestyle will you need to find out?

→ If the project is a commercial one, what aspects of the client's business will you need to find out?

→ Consider your responses to the above questions. What useful information can you deduce from the questions you have asked? Consider how this information might be used to inform your subsequent design solutions.

Understanding the Space

Spaces enclosed by building elements (floors, walls, ceilings, roofs) are the essential raw materials of interior design. Once a proper comprehension of the job has been reached through the process of brief taking and design analysis, it is necessary to understand the space. There are two different aspects of the space that are worthy of our attention: firstly, the spatial relationships that exist between the enclosed volume and the building elements that form the enclosure, and secondly, the construction of those building elements.

As with other parts of the design process, you should not view the job of getting to grips with the space as separate and distinct from other tasks. As your design evolves over time, so will the spatial relationships that exist within the project. They will change and develop, and it may be necessary to revisit and revise your understanding of how they work.

This chapter looks at how you can begin to read spaces through the use of drawings and models, and also through the wider use of drawing in the design process.

3.1

3.1

Chae-Pereira Architects in Seoul, South Korea, designed the interior of this wine bar and restaurant. The clever use of partitions divides the space and allows light to permeate while providing discrete areas for customers.

Understanding spatial relationships

—

Even when you are fortunate enough to have experienced a project space firsthand, it is unlikely that you will have had enough time to get to know it intimately. When working in a studio environment with no physical experience of the space, you need a methodology that allows you to connect in an intellectual sense with the space. Universally, designers draw and create models to give them this experience of a building.

All types of drawings can be made or used by a designer to help the process of understanding a space, from simple sketches to technical drawings. Technical drawing is a means of representing a three-dimensional space or object in two dimensions in such a way that dimensions, proportions, and relationships between different parts of the whole are clearly and accurately recorded. Any space or object will usually be described by using more than one drawing, often a combination of a plan and elevations and/or sections.

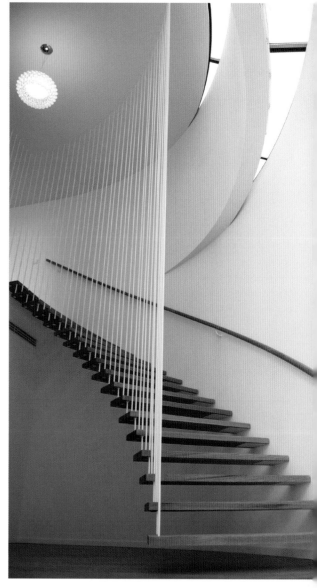

3.2

Before embarking on design work, the designer must fully understand how the spaces fit together and the way in which these spaces are affected by light throughout the day. Chae-Pereira Architects designed the Godzilla house in Seoul, South Korea. This staircase appears to hang from the ceiling, which produces a dramatic effect. By using white vertical rods, the designers were able to maximize the space and create a light and airy aesthetic.

3.2

54

Understanding through drawing

—

Technical drawings form a common language used by architects, designers, and engineers, though there are some differences in the way that the disciplines portray some details, and users should allow for this when reading the drawings. A space can only be fully described by using more than one drawing, often a combination of those that show the horizontal (plans) and the vertical (sections or elevations).

Technical drawings may depict spaces accurately, but they do not always show them in a way that we are used to seeing them. Because of this, they can appear cold, unnatural, and somewhat daunting to the uninitiated, but through practice most people will become comfortable with reading them and will appreciate them for the information that they contain and communicate.

Drawings are often amended and added to over time to reflect the development of a design, but initially they will be used to gain a feeling for the space. It is important to realize that although reading a drawing that already exists will go a long way to informing you about the space, the most complete understanding comes when the drawing is actually created by you, the designer. And the experience will be stronger still if you have undertaken the measured survey that precedes the making of the drawing. It is the hands-on approach that gives us the most complete knowledge of the space.

The process of drawing, where each measurement and the placement of each line is carefully considered, intensifies the relationship that the designer has with the space; it gives a more intimate understanding of a building. The act of drawing also gives time for reflection, which leads to an understanding of the possibilities that the building possesses.

Accurate technical drawings are based on carefully measured surveys. All relevant dimensions are taken on-site and noted in sketch form. These survey notes are then used in studio to create the scale drawings. Ultimately, what detail is shown in the drawings will be partly dictated by the scale at which they are drawn, but the survey should account for every possible dimension that might be needed to produce the drawings. Making a photographic record of details will also prove useful when creating the drawing at a later date.

Case study: **Construction drawings**

Construction drawings are technical drawings that are used to communicate a level of detail that will allow your design to be realized by a contractor or trade supplier.

They generally consist of a set of layout drawings, which show the overall design; component drawings, which show the key components of the design; and detail drawings, which show the materials, junctions, and fixing types you intend to use.

The drawings in this example are for a bespoke kitchen and dining area in a house conversion in Brighton, UK. They are clear and concise, and are drawn using a popular CAD (computer-aided design) package. Such drawings need not be complex, but they should clearly show your design intentions. In these examples, a simple tone has been added to aid legibility.

3.3

This plan shows the layout for a domestic kitchen. The principal components of the design and their positions and relationships within the space are clearly depicted. The materials are shaded to aid legibility.

3.4

This drawing details the construction of one of the kitchen cabinets in the design. Tone has been added to aid legibility.

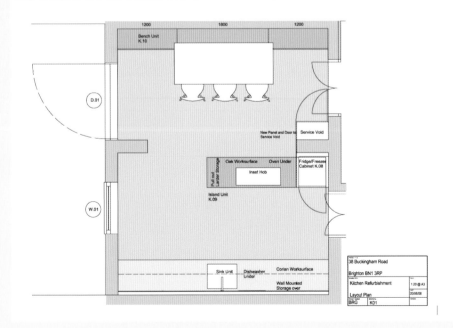

3.3

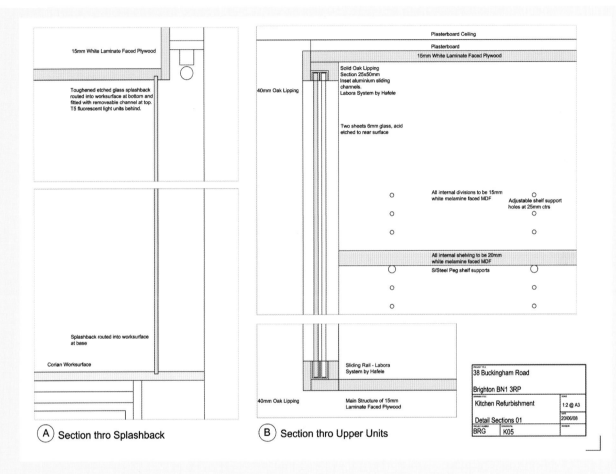

15mm White Laminate Faced Plywood

Toughened etched glass splashback
routed into worksurface at bottom and
fitted with removeable channel at top.
T5 fluorescent light units behind.

Splashback routed into worksurface
at base

Corian Worksurface

Plasterboard Ceiling

Plasterboard

15mm White Laminate Faced Plywood

Solid Oak Lipping
Section 25x50mm
Inset aluminium sliding
channels.
Labora System by Hafele

40mm Oak Lipping

Two sheets 8mm glass, acid
etched to rear surface

All internal divisions to be 15mm
white melamine faced MDF

Adjustable shelf support
holes at 25mm ctrs

All internal shelving to be 20mm
white melamine faced MDF

S/Steel Peg shelf supports

Sliding Rail - Labora
System by Hafele

40mm Oak Lipping

Main Structure of 15mm
Laminate Faced Plywood

(A) Section thro Splashback

(B) Section thro Upper Units

PROJECT TITLE 38 Buckingham Road		
Brighton BN1 3RP		
DRAWING TITLE Kitchen Refurbishment	SCALE 1:2 @ A3	
Detail Sections 01	DATE 20/06/08	
PROJECT NUMBER BRG	DRAWING No. K05	REVISION

3.4

3.5

This sketch provides a simple representation of the
units, showing the basic arrangement and forms.

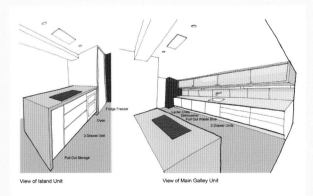

Fridge Freezer

Oven

3 Drawer Unit

Pull Out Storage

Larder Dishwasher
Pull Out Waste Bins

3 Drawer Units

View of Island Unit

View of Main Galley Unit

3.5

57

Understanding through models

—

Models are a three-dimensional method of visualizing a three-dimensional space. The word "model" implies a carefully constructed scale representation of a space. Some models do fit this description, but others can be very simple "sketch" models constructed from thick paper or other craft materials and adhesive tape in a matter of minutes. It doesn't matter how well finished the model is, it's more important that it captures the essence and spirit of a space and helps you to visualize the three-dimensional reality that you are trying to understand. Models can be made to a very high standard, but this is generally only for presentation purposes.

Like drawings, models can be amended over time to represent changes to the design, and the process of constructing a model, however rough it may be, will help you to understand how the space works, and how the different planes and surfaces meet and interact. Sketch models are almost infinitely adaptable. Openings can very quickly be cut to represent new windows, doors, or staircases. Pieces of paper can be taped in place to suggest new ways of dividing spaces. The sketch model should be treated like a sketchbook; it is a physical way to get ideas out of your head and into some sort of reality where they can be more readily assessed, compared, and shared. This is a very important technique, and one that designers should make use of as much as possible. As with sketching, you do not need to be embarrassed about your abilities with paper, scissors, craft knife, and tape; it is much more important that you simply use the technique. The use of basic materials and fixing methods, such as drafting tape or pins, adds to the spontaneity of the process and helps in the ready appreciation of structural changes and interventions. The process of manufacture tells you as much about the space as subsequent study of the model.

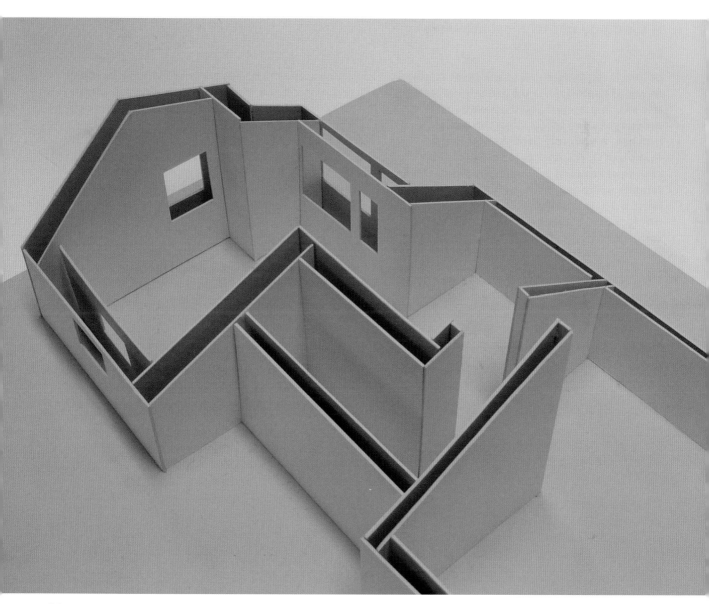

3.7

3.7

This model does not attempt to realistically portray decorative finishes. The uniform appearance of the card, from which it has been made, focuses attention on the space.

59

A typology of technical drawing

—

Before discussing some of the most common forms of technical drawing in interior design, it is worth emphasizing that technical drawing is used throughout the design process. It is simply because this is the first point in the design process at which technical drawing is encountered that the following exposition of drawing is placed here. It could equally well have come at other points of this book; indeed, drawing is referenced in Chapter 8, when presentation drawings are examined in more detail.

The three most basic technical drawings that we might use are plans, elevations, and sections. All three are scale drawings and are therefore accurate representations of the proportions of spaces in either the horizontal or the vertical plane.

Scale in technical drawing

—

Only occasionally do we draw the subject of a technical drawing at its full size. For interior designers, this might be feasible and necessary when showing details of part of a scheme (for example, how two different materials are treated, or "detailed" at their junction), but clearly it will never be possible to show a complete interior at full size. Most drawings, therefore, represent the subject at some fraction of their true size. The "scale" of the drawing indicates the ratio between a single unit of length on the

drawing and the equivalent "real-life" measurement. It is most usually expressed on the drawing as that ratio, for example, 1:25, where one centimeter on the drawing represents 25 centimeters in the actual space. Less commonly, it might be expressed as a fraction—for example, 1/25—where each unit of measurement on the drawing is shown at one twenty-fifth of its actual size (though, essentially, these are two different ways of saying the same thing). Scale is sometimes represented graphically on the drawing as a "scale bar." Because it is so easy to casually photocopy drawings and either reduce or enlarge them in size at the same time (and therefore change the scale), the scale bar can be very useful as there is always a visual, as well as a numerical, representation of scale on the drawing.

Scale rules are used to facilitate accurate plotting and measuring at scale. The rule comes ready marked with a linear representation of distance at various scales, so no calculations need to be made to change real-life size to paper size, or vice versa.

Rules can be marked in metric units (millimeters or meters, as appropriate), or in feet and inches. In this latter case, the scale ratio will be expressed as "x inches to the foot" (for example ½" = 1' 0", which is a ratio of 1:24).

Choosing a scale

—

There is no right or wrong scale to use for a drawing. The aim is to show the maximum amount of detail possible in the space, and therefore the most appropriate scale will usually be the one that neatly fills the space available on the drawing paper that is being used. When drawing manually, the scale needs to be decided before drafting begins. When drafting using CAD software, the drawing scale can usually be set prior to printing the finished drawing onto paper. Whatever scale is ultimately chosen, it should be clearly stated on the drawing, and because of the possibility of uncontrolled enlargements or reductions being made outside of the drawing office, it is good practice to state paper size in addition to the scale, for example 1:25 @ A3 or ½" to 1' @Arch B.

This list shows some metric and inch/foot scales used for interior design drawings. It is clear that common inch/foot scales are similar to, but not precisely the same as, common metric scales.

The largest scale shown (1:10) might be used for showing construction details or similar. The other scales could all be used for drawing plans, elevations, and sections to describe spaces from small rooms to entire floors of large buildings.

When it is necessary to show construction details for bespoke work, it might be appropriate to draw at full size, or a scale of 1:1. In some instances, details might be enlarged to show clearly how they are to be constructed. A scale of twice full size would be written as 2:1.

Common metric scales	Common inch/foot scales	Actual metric equivalent
1 : 10	1" = 1'	1 : 12
1 : 20	¾" = 1'	1 : 16
1 : 25	½" = 1'	1 : 24
1 : 50	¼" = 1'	1 : 48
1 : 100	⅛" = 1'	1 : 96

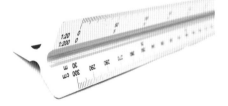

3.8

3.8

This is a metric scale rule and shows the scales 1:20 and 1:200.

The plan

—

Plans are simply maps and generally show the extent of one floor or level within a building, and they may only show a single room. Separate plans will show other floors or levels. They show detail within the room that can be drawn at scale, and many details are coded into symbols that should be easily recognizable to anyone with some experience of reading plans.

The convention is to show on plan all detail that would be visible if the space was cut horizontally at approximately one meter above the floor level, with the top section removed. All structure and objects that are wholly or partially below this level are shown on the plan drawing in their entirety. For example, a two-meter-high cabinet that sits on the floor is drawn as if viewed whole from above, and not as if it has been cut in half horizontally by the one-meter cut. Objects that are wholly above one-meter level may be shown on the plan, but will be delineated in a different style of line to objects below the one-meter level to aid the legibility of the drawing (usually a broken or "dashed" line).

The one-meter cut is not, however, absolute; common sense should prevail when deciding what is and what is not shown in the plan. For example, it would be unreasonable and misleading to omit windows from a plan just because the windowsill was at a height of 1300mm (1.3 meters or 4.3 feet) above floor level. It would be just as inappropriate, though, to include clerestory-style windows that were, for example, 600 mm (0.6 meters or 23.6 inches) tall, but which were positioned directly below ceiling level. You should take care to show everything that you think appropriate. However, you shouldn't expect that the plan by itself could tell the whole story. When two-dimensional drawings are used to describe three-dimensional space, a combination of plan (representing the horizontal plane) and elevations and/or sections (representing the vertical plane) will be used to portray all the features of that space, and they must always be read concurrently.

Drafting (the process of drawing) can employ different conventions of line weight and style to try and convey information; wider lines can be used to delineate structure, and lines can be softened by freehand drawing to represent upholstered furniture, for example. Annotations can also be added to drawings to highlight features that would not otherwise be entirely clear. North points are shown to aid orientation, and drawings are carefully titled and labeled in order to instantly identify them. These small points are important; carefully crafted and easily legible drawings promote confidence and convey a sense of professionalism to others using the drawings.

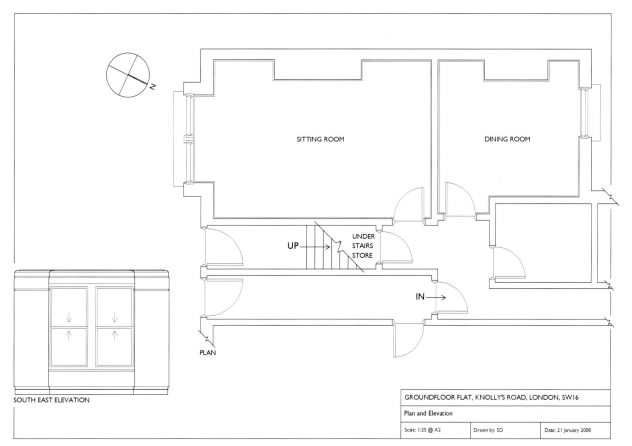

SITTING ROOM

DINING ROOM

UP →

UNDER
STAIRS
STORE

IN →

PLAN

SOUTH EAST ELEVATION

GROUNDFLOOR FLAT, KNOLLY'S ROAD, LONDON, SW16		
Plan and Elevation		
Scale: 1:25 @ A2	Drawn by: SD	Date: 21 January 2008

3.9

3.9

This survey drawing for a flat in London shows a floor
plan and an elevation of one of the walls. Note the title
block showing relevant information, such as drawing
scale and date of drafting, and other symbols on the
drawing such as the north point. As this is a survey
drawing of the building structure, no furniture is shown.

The elevation

—

Plans play an important role in interior design as they are usually the first tool used during space planning. However, in the same way that plans should not be read in isolation, the planning process must work in the vertical as well as the horizontal. A study of plans that show furniture layouts and structural elements will soon show that plans in themselves can be drawn entirely correctly but can still be misleading in their representation of space. The process of space planning must consider the impact of the vertical almost as soon as work on the horizontal plan is begun, and for that it is necessary to draw elevations and/or sections.

Where plans show horizontal surfaces, elevations show vertical ones. In other respects, they are very similar; they represent a record of height and width and are drawn to scale. As with other technical drawings, they do not represent the space as we see it in real life, but they are an ideal way to assess the proportions of elements such as walls, windows, doors, or fireplaces. They give a good understanding of spaces when used together with plans. The conventions employed when drawing elevations are similar to those used for plans. The vertical cut is taken one meter in front of the wall to be depicted, and all furniture and objects that sit closer to the wall than this line are shown in the elevation.

Once again, the furniture is not shown as if it has been cut in two; the complete piece is shown even when parts of the piece extend further from the wall than the one-meter cut line. As with the plan, there is some flexibility in what is shown and how it is depicted. Clarity is the key. Unlike the plan, an elevation does not show walls, floors, and ceiling structures. Instead, the elevation ends at the face of the boundary-building element (i.e. it ends at the walls, floor, and ceiling). As such, internal elevations show single spaces (multiple spaces are shown using sections). There must be a total absence of linear perspective in the elevation. This is relatively easy to understand when looking at a completed elevation but often difficult to master when drawing one. Many people experience the temptation to add illicit glimpses of perspective to their elevations, more so than doing the same to their plans. It is not clear why this should be so, but it may have to do with the fact that we naturally feel disconnected from the plan (it is only very occasionally going to be a view that we come close to seeing in real life), but we have a natural affinity with the elevation (a view we think we see almost all the time).

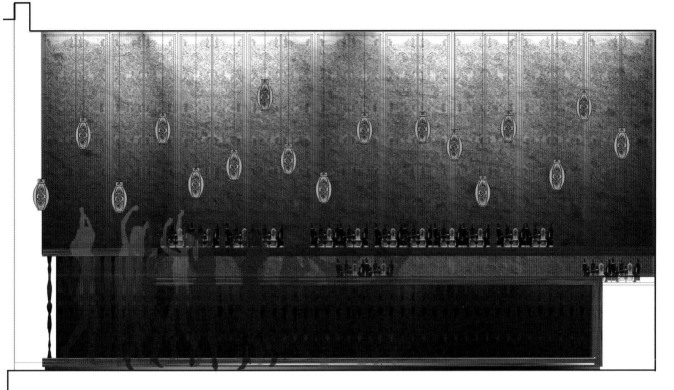

3.10

3.10

This elevation drawing shows part of the bar
area in a hotel in Bangalore, India. The rendering
gives an indication of material finishes, colors,
and proposed lighting effects. Figures have been
added to give a sense of scale and to animate the
drawing of what should in real life be a bustling
and lively space. This has helped to counter the
naturally static feel of technical drawings.

65

The section

—

The section works in the vertical plane as does the elevation but with one important difference. A section can be placed at any distance away from the wall that is the subject of the drawing, thus including or excluding features at will. In fact, the cut does not even need to be a single planar cut through the space; it can jump from plane to plane, varying in distance from the subject wall but remaining parallel to it. Like the elevation, there should be no perspective; but unlike the elevation, the structure enclosing the space is shown at the point where the section cut dissects it, so wall thicknesses and so on are indicated. Consequently, multiple rooms or spaces can be shown in their true relationship with one another.

3.11

This section drawn by Sarah Nevins, a student at Manchester School of Art, UK, for her final project, shows a center for urban cyclists. The drawing clearly illustrates the atmosphere of the main spaces of the scheme—how they are related to each other together with vertical relationships and circulation.

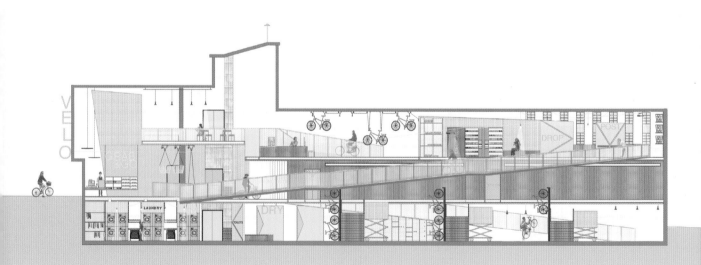

3.11

66

Thinking point: Manual or digital?

—

Are there any designers who still sit at their drawing boards to draw by hand? Can't all drawings be made by using drafting software on any good computer? And what about model-making—why would anyone want to work with glue, scissors, sticky tape, craft knife, card, and paper to make a model when they could use drafting software to produce a digital model of the space, which can be rendered and lit in an infinite number of ways? Isn't it sensible to tap into the power and freedom that computers give us for all our design work?

The answer is both yes and no.

There is no question that computers allow us to work smarter, more efficiently, and with more freedom than is often the case when using manual techniques. However, this argument misses a vital point about the relationship between old and new methods that can more than compensate for the efficiency that computers bring. Manual drafting and model-making is a craft that gives you a real connection with the project. There is a wonderful link that allows ideas to flow through you and your pencil onto the paper, which means you engage more fully with the project. All the decisions about placement of lines and so on belong to you, not a computer, so you are forced to think carefully about what you are drawing. There is no doubt that working manually leads to a better understanding of drawings, what they represent, and how they work. The manual process allows for a more expressive and spontaneous approach that computer-based design often lacks; a sweep of the hand across a sheet of paper that leaves a unique and eloquent pencil line is not something that can easily be reproduced by a computer.

On the other hand, computers give us the opportunity to copy and edit work quickly and easily. Simple functions, such as "copy and paste," are incredibly liberating—no more laborious hand drawing of 30 tables and 120 chairs on a restaurant plan, for example. Instead, after just a few keystrokes, the designer is free to concentrate on the design, rather than the act of drawing itself. Drawing with the computer also means that ideas can be exchanged quickly and easily by email or other means of file transfer. So, computers give us freedom and versatility throughout the design process, which is very appealing. But you should remember that the CAD software is essentially only a pencil; a tool to aid the drafting process. It has functions that enable some of the tedious aspects of working on drawings to be automated, and it can put lines onto a virtual sheet of paper where you tell it to, but CAD software cannot create a drawing by itself, nor is it able in most instances to decide if what is being drawn is sensible or logical in construction or space-planning terms. It is, therefore, important that the operator understands what it is that is being drawn and how it should be represented on the page. The computer cannot add creativity to a project: that is the sole responsibility of you, the designer.

Case study: Steel Lady House, South Korea

The Steel Lady House was constructed as a private commission in a luxury neighborhood in the center of Seoul, the capital of South Korea, by Chae-Pereira Architects. The site was challenging as it was narrow and had many other restrictions due to building codes, and the client required an area of some 300 square meters (3229 square feet) of space. Despite this, Chae-Pereira Architects created a spacious house with a series of internal spaces linked through a twisting, geometric internal staircase.

Externally, the house is a simple rectangular box that makes efficient use of the plot. This simple geometry is broken up by a diagonal grid cladding of stainless steel, which provides a link to the interior geometry and reduces the apparent scale. The interior of the house creates a wonderful contrast in terms of both the form of the spaces and the materials used. The main spaces respect the rectangular geometry but are punctuated by the organization of the circulation spaces, which take the form of a series of folded plate timber-veneered panels. This not only provides a dramatic intervention into the interior spaces but also creates a series of spaces that appear to contrast with the external form.

This use of dramatic folding forms, coupled with deep rich veneered panels, encases the spaces and provides a refuge from the external environment. The geometry draws people through the spaces as well as responding to the external light, which is diffused and refracted and provides contrast with the simple geometry of the main spaces. Areas such as the kitchen, dining, and living rooms are interlocking, forming a sequence of spaces that provide a variety of views.

The use of natural light is particularly important and this is used effectively to enhance the fractured nature of the panels but also to reinforce the rich timber used. This is supplemented by a simple system of artificial lighting, which is integrated into the panels.

3.12

Externally, the Steel Lady House has a simple geometry that responds to the site.

3.12

3.13

3.14

3.13

The interior of the house contains veneered
panels that add warmth and contrast to
the harder exterior of the building.

3.14

The timber-clad staircase forms
a dramatic intervention.

Interview: Chae-Pereira Architects

Laurent Pereira is the principal of Chae-Pereira Architects. They designed the Steel Lady House and are based in Seoul, South Korea.

Externally the building appears quite simple in its form, which is in contrast to the internal spaces. How did this develop through the design process?

→ The shape of the house is due to several factors; the pressure of maximizing construction against a strict code, which comes with the client's brief. This basic predetermined shape was modified into an ambiguous form with layers of semi-reflective stainless steel. The house looks like a box but isn't, and every facade has a specific relation to the house's environment.

The interior spaces are quite sculptural and appear quite geometrically complex. What methods did you use to create these?

→ We made plenty of models, which is the way we tend to start everything. Large-scale models are used to generate plans, sections and computer models; these models are then made into physical models again. This really gives you a feeling for the space. Finally, a lot is decided on-site, because here we work so fast. It can be messy, but I like to be able to improvise a little; you have to understand and visualize the space very well to do that.

How do these spaces respond to your design concept and the clients brief? What methods did you use to communicate your ideas to the client?

→ There is not so much communication work but just a good process. We create large models, material boards, and images to explore our own project visually; the process is very explicit, so we can show this material directly. It is essential to get the client's trust and support because there is so much competition for control in the construction process.

Were there any challenges with regards to the materials and construction of the project, such as the details and junctions? How did you overcome these?

→ Paradoxically, the most challenging is to get the correct concrete finish, where actually the teak veneer was the easiest. We wanted to create a house of layers: a metal box, then inside a concrete box, then a wood box, when you are in the house it is very clear.

As always, maintaining quality in the interior details took a lot of effort; the geometry looks complex, but we made sure that the junction details were simple and consistent. We worked really hard on-site to maintain the quality, which really paid off in the finished project as we attained a high level of finish.

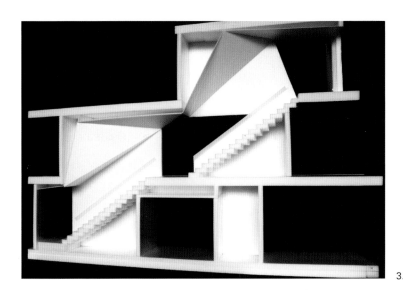

3.15

As shown here, the design for the Steel Lady house was developed with the extensive use of models.

3.15

Activity

—

01. Source some technical drawings of different spaces made by different designers—ideally ones that show furniture layouts. You could contact some designers and ask to see copies of drawings, or you may find drawings online.

→ Which conventions (ways of showing things) are the same between the different drawings?

→ Which conventions are different?

→ How well do you think the different drawings communicate the designer's intent for the space?

02. Consider how well any written notes or annotations add to the information communicated by the drawings.

→ Is there any difference in the way that soft and hard materials have been depicted?

→ Does the way that these materials have been shown help or hinder your understanding of the space?

Understanding Building Structures

Besides familiarizing yourself with the plan form of the space, you should try to make yourself aware of the methods used in the construction of the building. Understanding construction is not simply an academic exercise; knowing how a building is put together is a lesson in possibilities. Once you have a good idea of the structure, you will find it easier to make decisions relating to the implementation and practicality of your design work, especially when looked at in conjunction with the constraints incumbent upon the project, be they time, budget, legal, or technical.

A study of building construction will often change the way you look at the buildings that you use on a daily basis, and an enquiring eye is a very useful skill to develop. The knowledge that you gain by looking at structures will add greatly to your projects and, just as importantly, being able to speak with a degree of confidence about structure will give you credibility with contractors and clients alike. Unfortunately, details of the building structure are often hidden away underneath surface finishes and detailing. In the absence of definite information regarding its construction, experience will help you make some reasonable assumptions or deductions about the building.

4.1

4.1

The Welsh Assembly in Cardiff, Wales, is constructed from slate, timber, and glass and was designed by the Richard Rogers Partnership. This view shows the lobby and the dramatic ceiling and funnel. Sustainable materials were used throughout the building, including the timber used for the ceiling and funnel.

Building construction principles

—

All buildings have forces and loads imposed upon them. To remain standing, the building structure must be strong enough to resist the loads and not collapse. The building does this by providing a pathway through the structure for the loads to be safely transmitted to the foundations, the point of contact with the ground beneath the building.

The loads are usually classified as:

→ Dead loads: these are the loads placed on the structure by the weight of the materials used in its construction. All materials contribute to the total load, but traditionally the roof structure would make up a major portion of these loads.

→ Live (or superimposed) loads: these loads are imparted on the structure by any additional physical element placed in or on the building, for example, furniture and people, or snow upon the roof.

→ Wind loads: when acting upon the side of a building, winds can exert huge forces that must be borne by the building and safely transmitted through the structure to the foundations.

→ In some locations, buildings may on occasion be subject to seismic loads that need to be dealt with alongside the other loads and forces.

The structure of almost every building can be described in one of two ways: they are either frame (sometimes called "post-and-beam") structures or load-bearing (sometimes called "masonry") structures.

Framed structures

—

Framed structures are essentially a collection of horizontal beams (forming each floor level) that transmit forces to vertical columns. These columns, in turn, provide a pathway through which the forces can travel downward to the foundations and from there into the ground. The vertical columns may form the walls at the perimeter of the building or they may be distributed throughout the space. Where they are part of a wall structure, they will be covered with suitable materials to create the finished walls. When positioned within the space, two or more columns may be joined to create internal divisions or they may be left as discrete columns. The great benefit of this multilevel framework is that, because the columns are transmitting the loads vertically, solid wall structures are not needed to support the floors above and can therefore be omitted (creating large open-plan spaces punctuated by the supporting columns), or walls can be created using nonstructural materials such as glass. Framed structures allow us to build high-rise buildings that are often characterized by facades apparently composed entirely of glass, though the materials used for these curtain walls (that are mechanically suspended off the frame) can be practically anything. Radical architects of the Bauhaus movement in Germany in the 1920s first conceived the use of glass in this innovative way. Because of the strength of framed structures, buildings can be made very tall. It was the development of framed structures in the latter part of the nineteenth century that lead to the first high-rise buildings.

If the internal divisions are not carrying any load (other than their own weight), they can be moved or altered without the need for any significant interventions to the surrounding structure in order to maintain its integrity. For the designer, therefore, framed structures can give a lot of freedom in planning spaces.

Lightweight frames

Framed structures do not need to be large scale. The principle can just as easily be applied to houses as it can to skyscrapers. Lightweight timber frames are a common method of construction in many regions of the world, though the frame is usually invisible under a skin, or veneer, of other materials such as timber weatherboarding or brick. Frames of this type will usually be braced to prevent twisting by the addition of a plywood skin to the outside of the frame. Timber framing of residential developments allows fast and accurate construction by a relatively low-skilled workforce, as it is an easy material to work with; sections of the frame can be prefabricated off-site under better working conditions, then delivered to site for rapid assembly.

Timber frames are also an environmentally acceptable construction method, assuming that the timber used is from a sustainable source. Highly energy-efficient buildings can be made by inserting insulation between the vertical and horizontal timbers, creating buildings that perform extremely well in some of the most extreme climates, such as the northern hemisphere winters of Canada and Scandinavia. Light frames can also be made from thin section steel, galvanized to prevent corrosion. The internal face of the frame can be very easily covered in plasterboard/drywall or other materials to provide a surface suitable to receive decorative finishes.

4.2

4.2

The framed structure of The Farnsworth House by Mies van der Rohe in Plano, Illinois, USA, is clearly expressed here. It is a major visual element of this iconic design that is considered by many to be one of the most beautiful buildings ever designed. Not all framed structures display the frame so openly; many will be hidden.

Load-bearing structures

—

In a load-bearing structure, it is the masonry construction of the walls themselves that takes the weight of the floors and other walls above; in fact, the term "masonry construction" is often used to describe this type of structure. The walls therefore provide the pathways through which forces travel down the structure to the foundations. There is no separate constructional element of the building to do this, as with the frame in a framed structure. Care must be taken when adapting existing load-bearing elements of a structure to ensure that integrity is not compromised. If changes are made to the structure without adequate precautions being made, then the structure will at best be weakened, and at worst collapse.

If one wants to move door or window positions, or make new openings in a wall for whatever reason, then the loads that are being supported by the wall must be diverted to the sides of the opening to prevent collapse. This is usually achieved by the insertion of a beam or lintel at the top of the opening. This lintel will carry the loads traveling through the wall into the structure at the side of the opening, from where they will travel downward and so maintain the integrity of the structure. The beam or lintel itself will need to be adequately supported at both ends within the remaining structure. A lintel is a single, monolithic, component and can be manufactured from any suitable material; timber, stone, concrete (either reinforced or prestressed), or steel are the most common. Prestressed concrete lintels can span considerable distances, as can rolled steel joists (RSJs), which are often used in renovation work to allow the removal of internal walls by supporting the structure above.

If greater distances need to be spanned, it may be more appropriate to construct an arch rather than use a lintel, and this was certainly true before new technologies allowed the use of steel and concrete. Because of their superior mechanical properties, arches can generally support greater loads than lintels. An arch is considered as a single unit, but unlike a lintel it can be composed of a number of shaped components (usually stone or brick, called "voussoirs"), though it, too, can be monolithic, like a lintel. Once the individual elements of the arch are in place, the compressive forces (weight) of the building materials above hold them together. The simplest shape of arch is the round or semicircular arch, but there are many variations of form, even flat arches (sometimes called "jack arches"). Arch construction is a very practical engineering solution to the problem of spanning openings that are often treated as decorative elements of a building's facade.

Variations

—

Although the principles outlined above are relatively simple, experience will soon show that there are many variations on these themes that are used throughout construction. Manufacturers develop new methods and interpretations of existing solutions, and the desire of architects to challenge existing ideas of what a building is mean that these techniques soon become feasible. Changes to building regulations and codes for reasons of fire safety, better acoustic performance, reduced environmental impact, and so on, all mean that there is a need for new building practice. Details change, but the principles remain the same. With experience, it becomes easier to discern the theory behind the construction, but it is worth bearing these complexities in mind when looking at building structure.

4.3

4.3

During the design process, it is important to consider the implications of your decisions during the construction phase. In this site, a new opening has been created for a staircase and the required supporting structure can be clearly seen along with the initial structure for the staircase, which has been fixed to allow works on the opening to be completed. The work has been fully coordinated so that the new supporting steelwork has been calculated to adequately support the staircase without being visible once the work has been completed.

Materials for construction

—

In the same way that new ideas about buildings bring new methods of construction, they also inspire new materials. The range of materials that may be utilized during the construction process is much wider today then even a couple of decades ago, yet there remains a core of enduring materials, some of which have been around for centuries, which in one form or another account for the majority of building materials consumed.

Timber

—

Timber is a very convenient material to use for construction. It is easy to transport and handle, and it is generally easy and forgiving to work with. There are two categories: hardwood and softwood. It should be understood that these names are not intended to describe the actual properties of the timber; rather they refer to its origin.

Softwood is predominantly from coniferous trees, such as larch, pine, and spruce; it is often farmed in managed forests. It is generally used for construction (for example, light timber frames) and therefore usually hidden from view. However, it can be used decoratively, too.

Hardwood species are broadleaved trees, such as oak, ash, walnut, and teak. They are most often used decoratively for floors, furniture, and interior fittings. However, their timber may be used to construct heavy timber frames along traditional lines. Hardwoods are sometimes farmed from sustainable sources, but tropical hardwoods, such as teak, iroko, and wenge, are vulnerable to illegal logging operations in their native forest habitats, and several species are recognized internationally as being either endangered or critically endangered as a result. A responsible designer will check the status of timber species before specifying.

Raw timber can be processed into products such as plywood, chipboard, and fiberboard. These materials retain many of the desirable properties of timber, such as their workability, but overcome some of the problems, imperfections, and natural defects that may manifest themselves when using natural timber. They are sometimes used for construction, but they can also be used for furniture manufacture and may be on display. If used in this way, clients may see them as inferior or fake, but they are valid materials to use, especially in contemporary schemes, and their benefits can make them the most appropriate material choices in many situations.

4.4

4.4

When designing The National Assembly of
Wales, in Cardiff, the Richard Rogers Partnership
used timber very creatively. Here, Western Red
Cedar, a sustainable timber, was used to create
a curved ceiling that dominates the building
and creates a tremendous visual impact.

Stone

—

Stone is used in construction and many types are considered attractive enough to be used for their decorative as well as their practical properties. However, natural stone should be selected carefully as many types (limestone, for example) can be porous and could stain easily; they can also be relatively soft, such that they may not be suitable for uses such as flooring. When using stone, the suppliers' recommended fixing methods and after-care regime should always be followed. The surface can be cut and finished in different ways to highlight color, pattern, and texture. Designers should alert clients to the fact that, as a natural material, installed stone may not completely match any samples that have been previously viewed, as there may be significant variations in pattern or color, even from stone quarried at the same time and in the same location. Although relatively little energy is used to finish stone to a usable condition, it is not a sustainable material simply because once quarried, the source cannot be renewed. Indeed, designers are already finding that some quarries are exhausted of particular types of stone.

Brick

—

Brick is manufactured from clay that is hardened by kiln firing. The mineral content of the clay will define the color of the fired brick, which may vary from dark brown, red, or yellow. Surface texture can be applied to the molded or cut brick before firing. Standard sizes are used for construction, and brick can be used decoratively rather than structurally to clad interior and exterior surfaces.

Concrete

—

Concrete has been used as a building material for centuries. It is a mix of cement with an aggregate, traditionally stone chippings or gravel. Concrete is generally used in construction, where it is poured to form slabs for floors and foundations, or into molds (called "shuttering") to form vertical features such as walls or columns. It is often used in conjunction with steel reinforcing rods that combat tensile and shearing forces, but it is a very versatile material. It is increasingly used for its decorative qualities as it can be polished and colored. The gravel aggregate can be exposed, or other materials (such as crushed recycled glass) may be substituted, which give new opportunities for color and texture when the surface of the concrete is polished. However, the manufacture of cement used for concrete uses vast amounts of energy and produces a great deal of pollution, to the extent that many designers choose not to use the material because of the environmental harm that it causes. If used in large quantities in a structure, though, this damage may be offset by the thermal store effect of the mass of concrete, which helps to regulate temperature. Considered over a period of at least 15 years (depending on the installation), this can offset energy used during manufacture.

4.5

4.6

4.7

4.5

The washbowl in this bathroom is made from natural stone. Carefully detailed by the designer and expertly fitted, it lends an air of luxury and quality to the interior while also being a practical, hard-wearing, and decorative material.

4.6

In this contemporary take on the traditional deli, new shapes and styles of shop fittings are married to a use of materials that have been found in similar establishments for decades, giving a sense of connection with the past, and the natural markings of the marble provide subtle decoration.

4.7

Concrete can be treated in a number of different ways to create a decorative effect. For example, it can be textured and polished. Here, a rich, polished concrete finish was created for this fireplace. It creates a warm burnished focal point for this family room in a house in Fort Worth, Texas, USA.

Steel and other metals

—

Used in large amounts in the construction of the frames of many structures, steel is another material that is being used more for its aesthetic qualities. As always, careful selection of materials is important as there are different types and grades of steel suitable for different purposes. Decoratively, stainless steel is most commonly used for kitchen appliances, but other steels can be used for other purposes. Steel is available as sheets, bars, and tubes in various sizes. It can be formed into different shapes by metal fabricators. Architectural metal mesh is a relatively new treatment that has great decorative potential in which steel cable and rods are woven into sheets. Depending upon the weave and the gauge (size) of material used, the mesh may be completely rigid, or it may flex parallel to the warp and/or weft, allowing it to be wrapped around other objects and surfaces.

Other metals used both in construction and for their decorative qualities include aluminum, zinc, and copper. Designers should carefully consider the effects of oxidation on the visual appearance of these materials and protect against this as appropriate (or exploit it for decorative effect). Some metals are also relatively soft, so wear and tear needs to be considered, and there is also a possibility of electrolytic action between different metals in close proximity in humid or moist conditions (aluminum is especially prone to this), which may need to be researched before specifying.

Glass

—

Glass can be used as an interesting material in its own right, rather than simply being a practical choice of transparent material for windows. Glass has many uses, such as for shelving, work surfaces and splashboards, doors, screens, and wall panels. For any interior application, toughened or tempered glass should be specified, because such glass has been made safer by heat treating. Not only does this make it around five times stronger, it also affects the properties of the glass such that when broken it shatters in small square fragments which are far less likely to injure than long shards. However, once the glass is heat treated, it cannot be cut or worked, so any drilling or cutting required for hinges and handles must be done before the heat treatment takes place.

4.8

Here, glass has been used to create a partition between the sleeping and living areas. Using glass instead of a more traditional solid construction allows this studio room to feel light and spacious.

4.8

83

Mechanical and electrical systems

—

Buildings require systems to deliver heat, light, power, and water throughout the structure, and to take away waste. Although all but the end points of these systems are usually hidden from view, they do need to be considered by the interior designer as they require space within the structure, and this may impose limitations upon the design.

Climate control/water supply/electrical systems

—

Climate control is achieved in many ways, largely dependent upon location. Buildings in temperate climates may need systems for both cooling and heating; those in tropical climates may only require systems to cool the space. It is important to be familiar with the basic functions of these systems at the very least, as there is likely to be some evidence of their existence in the interior (heaters and radiators for example), and the siting and accessibility of the controls is an important consideration. Gas supply pipes for central heating and cooking appliances will have some restrictions placed upon their locations within the structure by building regulations. Depending upon the construction of the building, the installation or repositioning of these systems could be relatively straightforward, or it could be a major undertaking.

Water supply and drainage also require careful consideration. Supply pipes are relatively small in diameter, but drainage pipes are larger, especially soil pipes that take foul water from toilets. Building codes and regulations often place controls on where these can be positioned, which may impact upon options for planning bathrooms and the like.

Although electrical supplies have been built into houses for decades, many design projects now need to consider cabling for digital media such as televisions, phone, computer networks, and lighting controls. As with the other systems listed, cabling and power supplies can take up large amounts of space in walls, ceilings, and under floors, and they should be considered from the start of a project. Just as a designer would work with professional plumbers or air conditioning engineers, most would also subcontract the design of integrated data and electrical systems to a specialist. It is likely that the designer will have a large part to play in simpler installations of lighting and power systems, so once again it is sensible to have an understanding of the needs of these systems.

4.9

4.9

Normally out of sight, but no less important than any
visible element, are the building services such as
heating and air conditioning. The problems of integrating
unsightly air conditioning into the existing structure of
this bar have been cleverly solved by Nelson Designs.
A stretched vinyl material neatly covers the ductwork,
while providing a satisfying counterpoint to the brick.

Case study: Olson Headquarters, USA

The new Olson Headquarters in Minneapolis, Minnesota, was designed by Gensler—a firm of architects and designers. Olson is an innovative and leading provider of creative solutions and strategic thinking in the advertising and marketing sector. So, the new building needed to reflect their creative approach. One of the key requirements of the brief was to create clear communication through the interior and promote interaction for all that used the space: both clients and staff. Gensler provided a design solution for Olson's headquarters that is a catalyst for innovation and created a workspace that strengthens connections to clients and the community.

The building was originally a Ford Model A and Model T car assembly plant that used vertical assembly techniques with very large floor areas. The design team embraced the historic openings, structure, and exterior brick walls, along with new materials that would complement the existing building shell. Materials such as zinc, steel, reclaimed wood, and felt are left untreated and these assemblies are intentionally expressed, strengthening the concept of connections.

The design supports innovation by creating spaces that connect people. The staircase is the center of the agency and connects all levels of the space. Its four-story felt and mirror wall creates a series of unimagined views of the agency as you travel on the stairs. Digital displays, cultural artifacts, string art installations, and lounge spaces unfold around the stairs creating areas to gather and connect.

The work areas are designed for availability—change and reconfiguration are constant at Olson. The open office workstations move easily with a small kit of parts, while the private offices—made of demountable partitions—support flexibility.

Another key feature are the dedicated brand rooms for client and agency working sessions, which facilitate dialogue, pinups, and brainstorming through their interior treatments that seek to capture the values and personalities of the individual brands. Client pitch rooms are diverse, some are formal while others have a more relaxed interior style, and there are flexible spaces where people can gather; these areas allow for many different types of meetings.

4.10

4.10

The staircase creates a focal point with
displays of art and cultural artifacts.

4.11

4.11

Office areas provide flexible
spaces for meetings.

Interview: Gensler

Betsy Vohs is an architectural designer and senior associate at Gensler. Gensler is an integrated architectural design and planning company.

You started with an industrial building that had large floor areas. How did this shape your initial response to the project?

→ The approach to the large floor plates was to separate them into areas that clearly signify public and private space. The public spaces have the social areas, like the large interconnecting stairs, coffee bars, lounge spaces, and client meeting areas. The rest of the plan has areas for work with private internal meeting areas and collaboration zones.

Were any substantial structural alterations required to realize the scheme? Were there any problems with the existing structure?

→ This building is historic and the regulatory agencies required that the two original elevator shafts that carried the cars through the assembly line were to remain as vertical circulation.

These openings were in two challenging locations on the plan. We used one to house a large mirror-clad void that holds a steel-and-timber staircase, which connects the entire agency together through all four levels. The other was expanded to create a two-story atrium that is anchored by a gathering area and stage. This space holds all agency gatherings and concerts, and is a favorite meeting spot for a quick conversation among the creative talent.

How did you create strong vertical links in a principally horizontal structure?

→ This strong vertical link was critical to Olson's brief. They needed to create interaction between the different levels and between different groups within this large agency. So through the program distribution, we designed areas that were unique and special on each floor to draw people through the entire agency. These activities reinforce the idea of connection that is anchored by the central stairs, with its industrial materials and small pieces of mirror that create fractured views of the agency as you move through the space.

What was your philosophy behind the choice of materials for the project?

→ The materiality of the space is central to the experience and connection to Olson's brand. The historic nature of the building's past became a guide for the material choices and a way to make the space feel authentic to the building legacy. The key materials were industrial materials sourced locally and fabricated by local craftsmen. Some of the signature materials include steel, glass, mirror, rubber, felt, leather, and wool.

These are all materials found in early Model A and Model T cars that were produced in the factory. Reclaimed oak floors from Lake Superior were used throughout the space to create a warm horizontal plane that is in contrast to the raw materials of the stairs.

4.12

Crafts, such as stitching, were used to create interest and connection.

4.12

Activity

—

01. Think about the construction of your home.

→ Is it obvious which type of construction (framed or load-bearing) it is?

→ If not, consider how you might go about determining which type of construction has been used. What professionals might you need to consult to help you find out?

02. Visit a public space that you know well.

→ Can you identify the major categories of materials that are visible within the space?

→ Do they bring any decorative (or other) qualities to the space?

→ What practical issues can you think of that might apply to the upkeep and maintenance of these materials?

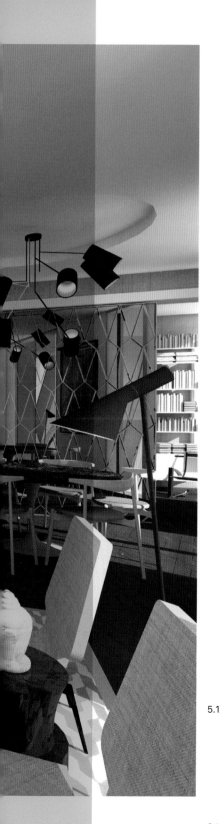

Organizing the Space

The brief has been taken, the raw data scrutinized and analyzed, research undertaken, and the space surveyed. A concept has been generated to drive the project forward and to give that reassurance of a reference point for the design. So now for the part of a project that most enthuses the majority of designers. The time when your imagination is given free rein to envisage unique and special solutions. It is the time when ideas take shape and become clearly defined, when nebulous ideas are made manifest and given body and form through your sketches and drawings.

Design principles are the axioms by which we can control and organize a space. They have been tested over time and have proven to be resilient and adaptable to the needs of different design disciplines. Many are universal: recognized across different cultures. However, as a designer, you should not be afraid to question them. It would, perhaps, be more appropriate to view the principles as guidelines—good solutions will usually be achieved by following them, but truly spectacular and inspiring results are sometimes only achieved by working contrary to the accepted ways. As with most disciplines, though, having a sound knowledge of the basics is needed before the rules can be broken successfully.

5.1

5.1

The furniture pieces shown in this computer-generated visual of a Docklands apartment in London, UK, by Project Orange, complement each other through the use of color and shape. They have been cleverly placed to make the best of the space and to create separate areas.

91

Design development

—

Development is the process of taking an idea, identifying its strengths and weaknesses, and resolving any problems to create a strong design solution. Designers almost universally conduct the development process through sketching; but note that the term "sketching" does not necessarily mean the creation of drawings with artistic merit. Rather, it is about the use of a sketchbook as a notebook, a place where ideas are visualized, and about the way in which sketching enables the designer to express an idea visually through the use of pen/pencil and paper. Sketching should be one of the fundamental design tools by which you create successful design solutions.

One of the most important points for the new designer to understand is this: you cannot conjure up a fully resolved and finished design solution in your head and use drawing only as a means to record the finished product. It is the act of drawing itself that will reveal to you the extent of a design problem, and only further drawing will allow you to find the best solution from among many possible solutions. At this stage of the process, designers draw to identify and resolve problems on the way to creating fully developed and resolved solutions. Remember that sketching is an exciting process. What unique and beautiful solutions will you create to answer the practical and aesthetic needs of the project?

5.2

5.2

This perspective sketch has been carefully drawn using simple techniques to accurately assess the current state of the proposed design solution. Shading has been added to improve the three-dimensional qualities of the drawing.

How to sketch

—

So, how should you approach the task of sketching if you have never tried it before? Equip yourself with one or more sketchbooks, or even a pile of paper from the photocopier. It does not matter what it is, and it does not matter what your sketchbook looks like (though a proper sketchbook will allow easy access to sketches and help establish a timeline for the development of your ideas). Sketchbooks should be kept available all the time so that you can quickly and easily jot down your thoughts, and never lose the germ of a great idea. Many designers have sketchbooks of different sizes in use simultaneously, each suited to a different purpose.

A small pocket-size book (perhaps A5 or half-letter size, or even smaller) is most useful for keeping with you at all times, though the small format makes it very much a tool for taking visual notes, rather than an easy platform for developing a design. Books at A4 (letter size) can be carried in a briefcase, laptop case, or a shoulder bag, and are a good compromise between portability and ease of sketching. Larger books (A3 or tabloid) are useful to keep in the studio, and though they may not be used as often, their larger format helps with freedom of expression when sketching. Spiral-bound books are easier to hold open when drawing, but hardbound books will often last better and are easier to file on the bookshelf. It really does not matter what you use, but do make sure you use something and keep on using it. Your sketching ability and confidence will improve through practice, even without formal training.

5.3

This sketch perspective is made carefully enough that proportions and planning implications can be assessed. It has been drawn quickly, which means that the designer can try out many ideas and options without becoming too precious about any of the ideas and unwilling to change.

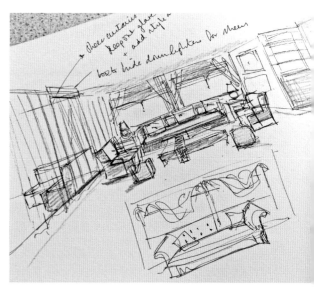

5.3

Tools for sketching

—

There is no perfect pencil or pen to use when sketching; you should experiment and find the one that gives you the most satisfying mark; for example, designers might use traditional wood-cased graphite pencils, modern mechanical or technical pencils, ballpoint pens, fiber-tip pens, or fountain pens. Probably the one instrument that is least suited to sketching is the technical pen. These should be kept for their proper purpose of drafting on tracing paper or film and not used in sketchbooks as pen nibs can get blocked with the fibers from the paper.

When beginning to sketch, students are often apprehensive about making marks on the pristine pages of a sketchbook, particularly if they feel they do not have a talent for sketching. This is a real shame, as one of the keys to producing informative (but not necessarily beautiful looking) sketches is having a confidence in mark-making that only comes through practice. To start sketching, gather together a variety of pens and pencils and simply draw shapes in your sketchbook. Try cross-hatching the shapes you have drawn. Do not aim for perfection and, if using a pencil, do not be tempted to erase any lines that you consider to be wrong—ignore them and carry on. Notice how the different pens and pencils feel in your hand, and the range of different marks they make. Which tool do you feel most comfortable with?

The softer grades of graphite pencils most often used for sketching make fluid, dynamic lines that express spontaneity and movement. However, their lines can be prone to smudging. They can have a finesse about them that is missing from other mark-making tools, and they allow subtle shading effects to be included in the sketch. Harder grades of pencil are not usually the most suitable for sketching as their fine, faint, lines do not encourage freedom of expression, and they can be difficult to see. They produce drawings that feel timid and mean. Ballpoint and fiber-tip pens are often a good choice. They make bold, strong shapes on the paper and express confidence. First-time sketchers are often hesitant about using pens and would rather use pencils, but pens should be tried before you decide which is going to be your preferred method of mark-making.

5.4

5.4

The addition of color to a sketch does a great deal to
help the visualization process. It helps the designer to
understand the implications of the decisions that have
been made regarding the color scheme, which should
be considered during the design development.

Practical tips for sketching

—

Sign and date all of the drawings you make in your sketchbook—from the very first seminal drawings to those that have developed the design in greater detail. This is helpful when you are reviewing your work, which is worth doing every so often, as a quick glance through old sketchbooks will remind you of ideas. More importantly from a business point of view, signed and dated drawings can prove to be a helpful tool should there ever be a dispute about the ownership of a design.

Get down on paper the first thoughts you have; do not dwell upon them before committing them to paper. Look at them, see their merits and problems, and sketch them again to see if you can make them better. Work with simple strokes; go over the drawing again and again; think about it or talk about it with someone else. At some point, you will know that you have solved most of the problems and have a good idea of how the design might work.

You will then need to start more accurate drawings (on the drawing board or with CAD) to make sure the design works. When things are drawn accurately in plan and elevation or section, you may realize that your initial ideas are not totally practical, so further work takes place on the drawing board. This is another point where manual drafting and sketching can be an easier way of taking the design forward. As ever, there is no single fixed way of proceeding, but various techniques are available to the designer. Many designers take a sheet of tracing paper large enough to cover the part of the drawing that needs resolving, lay it over the drawing, and sketch alternative ideas on to it, using the existing drawing as a guide. As one sketch is completed, the paper can be moved across the drawing to allow others to be made, until the problem is resolved.

These techniques for developing the design by drawing are used alongside an understanding of the principles discussed in the next section in order to create successful planning solutions.

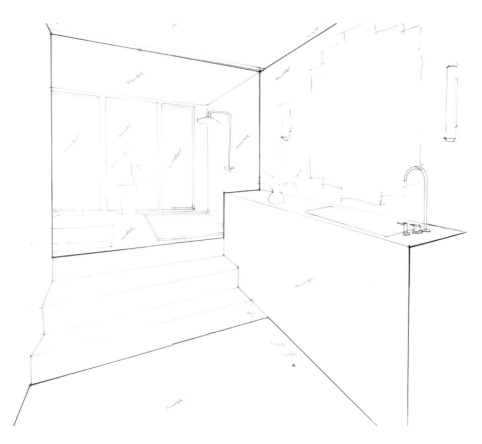

5.5

5.5

This is a loosely constructed draft sketch, but it still conveys the main themes of the design and helps the designer to develop ideas.

5.6

Through the use of color and tone, this sketch is developed to provide a clearer image of the ideas for the space. This helps viewers, such as the client, to understand the designer's intentions.

5.6

Human dimensions and scale

—

The one common denominator that lies behind all space planning is people. Whatever the function of the space, whatever the scale of the space, people are going to be a part of it. If that is so, then it is right that we take time to understand how people connect with the world around them.

Ergonomics

—

Ergonomics is about designing for people and their immediate physical needs, and as a starting point it uses anthropometric data that details the range and diversity of human dimensions. There are many books of design data that are potentially helpful, but interior design is a real subject with practical problems and practical solutions; therefore, it would be a mistake to rely on someone else's observations at the expense of making your own. For example, rather than working exclusively in plan and asking the question: "Is the access adequate?", take steps to visualize the situation for yourself and use a tape measure to confirm the required dimensions. Visualization of the problem could involve acting out a movement or action, creating a mock-up of your proposal by using props such as pieces of existing furniture, or using tape to measure out shapes of walls or pieces of furniture on the floor or against existing walls.

Always remember that you are an individual, just as the client is, so you may need to modify your measurements accordingly. If you are designing for a large and/or indeterminate group of people, be aware of extremes of the population such as the very young and old. It is also important to think about volume in addition to area: the circulation space between two relatively low items of furniture can be considerably narrower than that between two items where one or both of them are taller, without the access feeling restricted.

5.7

Remember that ergonomics does not just cover size; it also looks at how much effort is needed to perform a task. Think about an everyday action, such as opening a door. How easy or difficult this is will be a real indicator of the quality of a design. A hand taking hold of an object like a door handle is a fundamental connection with the space, and the experience that the user has will influence their perception of the building. How does the door handle fit the hand? Does it feel sturdy or not? Does it embody a feeling of quality or not? How much physical effort is required to turn the handle? Overall, does this simple experience of opening a door give a positive or negative message about the space? Even if the experience is a good one for you, how do you think it would be for someone who is 40 or 50 years older than you? Will they have a positive experience, or will the effort required of them be unreasonable?

If you are designing for one client, or a limited number of people, it might be appropriate to tailor the design solution to them closely, but this can exclude or disadvantage people who may subsequently use the space. As ever, there is not a right or wrong answer to this problem, but careful analysis should lead to a conclusion as to which approach is most appropriate.

5.7

Door handles are one of the points at which we physically connect with design. They should be easy to operate and hold, whether they turn or not, and the feel of the materials also needs to be appropriate to the rest of the design. This design was created by Based Upon.

Proxemics

—

The way in which we interact with other people is an expression of their status within our social group. Proxemics is the term used to describe the study of the way we interact with others. We keep a distance between ourselves in interpersonal situations, which is an expression of various cultural and social factors.

The anthropologist Edward T. Hall described the relationship of distance to status. He divided that relationship into four categories:

→ Intimate space: the smallest zone, where we embrace, touch, or whisper.

→ Personal space: the next smallest zone, which we reserve for conversation with close friends or family.

→ Social space: an intermediate zone, which allows for more general conversation and interaction with those whom we may consider as friends or acquaintances.

→ Public space: the largest zone, which accounts for all other interactions with people.

Hall defined these zones by measurement, but there is actually considerable variation in the size of these zones by culture, gender, and individual preference. We are innately aware of the effect of proxemics; most people feel uncomfortable in a lift or elevator with other people that they do not know, an effect more pronounced when it is full. Though not as extreme, the same feelings are experienced in any space, and so it is incumbent upon the designer to consider how these feelings can be moderated and allowed for. Providing more seats than are expected to be required in public spaces should ensure that anxiety about proximity to strangers is kept to a minimum. Try to put yourself in different situations and imagine how you might tackle them through your planning solutions, remembering that the client's reaction to a situation may not be the same as your own.

Scale

—

Measured (or mechanical) scale is the correlation between the actual size of an object and a standard system of measurement. Visual scale is a judgment we make about the relative sizes of objects and is not related to drawing scale described in the previous chapter. We are constantly and subconsciously comparing elements of the visual scene before us—is this chair small or large in relation to that one? Is that doorway small or large compared to the wall where it is positioned?

Human scale takes this desire to compare a stage further as it looks at the relationship between the dimensions of a space or object and their fit with the proportions of the human body. When something is scaled to fit or work easily with the human body, it can be said to be of human scale— examples could be a kitchen countertop or a flight of stairs. Sometimes buildings, furniture, and other elements of interiors we encounter are deliberately sized in opposition to the human body to provoke a response from us. Large spaces induce a sense of awe and wonder through their size, for example, but taken to extremes, this mismatch of scale could leave us feeling exposed and vulnerable. On the other hand, small spaces could feel welcoming and protecting, or they might feel claustrophobic.

5.8

Proxemics is a particularly important consideration when designing public spaces. This small grouping of chairs and table provide an everyday reference point that help the user feel comfortable within this open space.

5.8

Proportioning systems

—

Proportion is the relationship between one part (or parts) and the whole. It is the relationship between the parts of a whole that has been subdivided, of the vertical to the horizontal, the width to the depth, or the height to the length. It tells us whether something is thick or thin, wide or flat, tall or short. Proportion exists within an object (the relationship between the height to the width of a table, for example), or as part of a group of objects.

The brain naturally sees some proportional relationships as being more attractive than others, and we have discovered or invented many different proportioning systems to define and control proportional relationships as a result. Some of these systems are recent inventions; others have been in use for centuries and were well known to architects such as Andrea Palladio, who said that proportion is "harmony for the eyes."

Proportioning systems can be very helpful to the designer, but however comfortable it can feel to design with the authority of an established system to govern design decisions, the system used should not be held as sacrosanct. Throughout the design process, the designer needs to remain self-critical, and if the results of applying a particular proportioning system do not add anything to the design, then it should not be used purely because of a dogmatic belief in its inviolability. When Le Corbusier's assistants were struggling to apply the sensibilities of the Modulor scale (Le Corbusier's own creation) successfully to a building, they asked the architect what they should do. He simply said, "If it doesn't work, don't use it."

Proportioning systems exist to establish a consistent set of visual relationships between the parts of a design. Like the other design principles, proportioning systems are a method of formalizing the reasoning behind aesthetic decisions. Their implementation helps to unify and harmonize a set of disparate design elements, and so produce satisfying visual arrangements of building elements, furniture, accessories, and so on. Some of the most well-known proportioning systems are described here.

Golden section (or golden ratio)

—

Mathematically, the golden section is defined as the ratio 1:1.618. It might look mundane, but it is a ratio that surprises because of its universal popularity. It is seen by many people and cultures as a harmonious relationship between two unequal parts, and it is one that is found (at least approximately) in many instances in the natural world. A rectangle drawn with the length of its sides in accordance with the golden section has been used many times in art and architecture as the control for the proportions of the facade of a building or the composition of an artwork.

Golden rectangles are easily constructed: from the midpoint of one side of a square, draw a line to the opposite corner of the square. Use this as the radius of an arc, which can be struck from that corner until it intersects the extended side of the square. The point at which the arc and the extended side of the square meets defines the long side of the golden section rectangle (see diagram).

The ken

—

A system developed in Japan, the ken is still used to define room sizes in houses built in the Japanese tradition. The system uses the traditional floor mat—the tatami—as the basic unit. The mats are usually standard sizes of 90cm x 180cm (35in x 70in), though there is some variation depending upon the region of Japan from which the mats originate. Rooms are sometimes defined by the number of mats that cover the floor area. For example, tearooms are often four and a half mats in size, whereas shops used to be five and a half mats. Because it is based on a standard size of mat, it is an absolute measure, not just a proportion. There are rules and traditions that govern the patterns in which the mats can be laid out. The mats are never laid in a simple grid pattern, and they are arranged so that no more than two corners meet at any point.

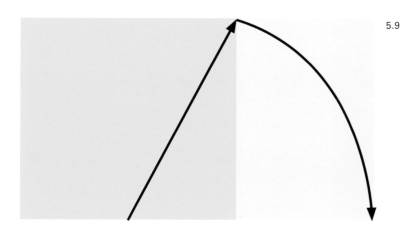

5.9

5.9

The golden section rectangle is relatively straightforward to construct and it can be used to define and regulate the proportions of many elements of a design.

The Modulor

—

The Swiss-born architect Le Corbusier developed his own proportioning system, which he based on three main measurements derived from the human figure, though it also draws heavily on the golden section and the Fibonacci numbers. The Modulor system has many other measurements that originate from the three main ones, and all of these measurements were used to define elements of a design—from the facades of buildings, through elements of the interior design, to the dimensions of sofas and chairs.

Manufactured sizes

—

This is a very practical proportioning system. It uses the sizes of ready-made materials to define the ratio of width to length. For example, plywood is typically supplied in standard sheet sizes, and these dimensions (or multiples of them) could define the size of details made from the material, such as wall paneling. Using manufactured sizes means that the use of materials is very efficient. When working with manufactured sizes, it is clearly important to research the options available before commencing the more detailed design work.

5.10

5.10

Le Corbusier used his own proportioning system, the Modulor, to regulate the internal and external dimensions of his Cité Radieuse/Unité d'Habitation.

Fibonacci numbers

—

This series of numbers has been known for centuries and was first described in the West by Leonardo of Pisa (also known as "Fibonacci") in 1220. The sequence begins with 0, followed by 1. Each subsequent number is the sum of the previous two numbers. Like the golden section, it appears in many instances in the natural world. A sequence of two, three, four, or more consecutive numbers can be drawn from any point within the series and used as regulators in a design. For example, drawer fronts often look well proportioned if the height of each drawer (from the bottom to the top of a cabinet) gets smaller, so a designer might choose to proportion the drawer heights in the ratio of 8 to 13 to 21.

"My own" ratio

—

It does not follow that you must use a recognized proportioning system to help create your design. You can create your own regulating dimensions. Whatever they are, repeated use throughout the visual composition will provide unity and strength to the design. You might choose, for example, to create built-in furniture using a standard panel width of 450mm (17 inches) with a shadow gap between panels of 5mm (0.2 inch). This standard size (or multiples of it) could be used to describe the entire visual identity of the piece or space that you create. Your design work can be aided by drawing, to scale, a grid based on these dimensions over which you can place tracing or layout paper. It is then very easy to sketch ideas and check their feasibility and practicality, which is all part of the development of the design.

5.11

0/1/1/2/3/5/8/ 13/21/34/55/ 89/144/233/ 377/610

5.11

Adjacent numbers from the Fibonacci series appear in many instances in the natural world and can be used to regulate elements of a design

Ordering systems

—

If proportioning systems exist to help us define sizes and ratios, ordering systems are there to help us collate a visually attractive three-dimensional composition using the building and all that we are placing inside it. It will involve manipulating the existing and proposed elements, and it is primarily concerned with the aesthetic, so judgments about the relative importance of this and the practical side of the design will need to be made.

The desire for a strong aesthetic solution may sometimes demand that an element is added to the overall composition that has no practical purpose within the scheme. When this is the case, the designer should not underestimate the power and importance of the aesthetic and should be prepared to do what is necessary for the integrity of the design. Application of ordering systems usually means that the designer's judgment will be used to decide at what point the optimum state is reached within the composition. This is one of those difficult-to-learn design issues, where there is no right and wrong, so it is important to try out different options (by drawing or other means) to ensure that the most favorable solution is reached.

Axis

—

This system uses an imaginary line to organize the whole, or parts, of the space. It is usually applied to the plan view of a space but could equally work in elevation. The organization of elements about the axis may be symmetrical or asymmetrical (this is explained later).

Balance

—

Each interior element has different properties—form, surface (texture), color, and size, for example. These need to be considered and arranged so that they balance with the same properties of other elements. The visual arrangement should be stable. This does not mean, though, that all things should be equal in size or placement, nor does it mean that the final composition will feel static. It is quite possible for the arrangement to be balanced and dynamic at the same time. There are different types of balance: symmetrical, radial, and asymmetrical.

Symmetrical balance works about an axis and suggests a mirrored arrangement of elements. Radial balance works around a center point or datum. Asymmetrical balance refers to the state of visual equilibrium achieved when elements of varying size, shape, color, and so on are arranged by careful consideration of their properties. More specifically, asymmetrical balance requires that strong visual elements are balanced by other less strong elements. Larger areas of more neutral colors may balance small objects or areas of strong color, for example. The careful distribution of "negative space" between the elements aids the composition.

5.12

5.12

In this restaurant at the South Place Hotel in
London, UK, designed by Conran & Partners,
a strong visual axis has been created by
the mirrorlike structure on the ceiling. It
helps to disguise the awkward effect that
the sloping wall has on this space.

Datum

—

This system uses a point or a center to arrange other elements of the composition. The datum could be an actual object or feature within the building structure and therefore visible, or it could be implied simply by the arrangement of furniture or other elements.

Harmony

—

Whereas balance seeks to achieve a visual congruity by careful placement of items that may not share properties of shape, color, and so on, harmony seeks to achieve a similar congress of parts, but it relies on the careful selection of elements that do share some common property.

5.13

5.14

Unity / variety

—

Remember that the principles of balance and harmony are just that: they are definitely not about uniformity. In all cases, we are talking about objects with numerous and multifaceted properties. It is possible to unify through a common property (material, color, texture, shape, location) and still retain variety in other aspects, generally leading to a more interesting design solution that avoids sterility.

Emphasis / dominance

—

A feature or element that is emphasized by some means becomes a focus for the space. Focal points give visual interest. They provide a point on which the eye can stop and take stock of the visual environment. As long as they are not too abundant, focal points describe a path that the eye can follow around a space, giving sense and order to an interior. Emphasis is often articulated through size, color, or shape, and this may be exaggerated to an unexpected degree to achieve emphasis. The placement of an object is also used for emphasis. Objects can be positioned at the end of an axis, at a datum, or they may be placed in opposition to the prevailing grid.

5.13

Harmony is created in this scheme through similarities in color and texture of different elements; the bust and the bed, and the rug and the wall covering, for example. At the same time, the contrast in the form and color of the chair avoids a stagnant scheme.

5.14

The designers have played with ideas of harmony, unity, and variety in this youth hostel café. The same style of chair is specified in different colors, and the simple shape of the chair echoes the regular lines in the graphic print of the telephone boxes behind.

5.15

The focus of this contemporary bathroom is the bath. The overhead lighting scheme emphasizes and reflects the importance of this feature. The choice of materials has been limited so that the marble around the bath, the fireplace, and the floor are in harmony to create a tranquil effect.

5.15

Rhythm / Repetition

—

Rhythm naturally makes us think of music, or rather the division of a musical piece into a regular, repeating, ordered pattern of sound. Rhythm in visual design has a similar effect. It refers to the use of repeating patterns, shapes, and forms, which are recognized by the viewer and interpreted as an ordering influence on the space. Simple rhythms can be created by repeating features, such as furniture or windows, and more complex and subtle rhythms can be promoted through the similarity of color, size, shape, and so on. Rhythms can build in layers with simple bass drum-like rhythms of larger elements augmented by more subtle "hi-hat" rhythms; for example, a pattern applied to a surface. Rhythms created in one medium can be echoed in another. Although we may only pick up on rhythms in a subconscious way, they provide visual measurement and punctuation of a space, the effect of which is to animate the space and to help it flow.

5.16

This hotel bedroom uses a sophisticated and muted palette of colors. These colors are not only used on the textiles on the bed, but they are also repeated in the furniture and in the surface decoration on the cupboards and walls.

5.16

5.17

Alternating horizontal and vertical staircase elements create a familiar and reassuring rhythm that is gently bolstered by the use of a uniform material (steel) for the handrail, balustrade, and stair edging detail to create a powerful but discrete composition. Hard edges are visually softened by the proximity of the books.

5.17

Thinking point: Zoning

—

If the functional requirements of the brief are such that the space will play host to more than one specific activity, the first step to achieving a planning solution is to look at the zoning of the space. This assessment will show which functions fit best in specific parts of the space, and it should be conducted in very broad terms, without any reference to specifics of furniture dimensions. Different zoning layouts should be tested, and by compiling lists of strengths and weaknesses for each zoning option, it should be possible to identify a preferred zoning proposal. This will then be taken as the basis for more detailed planning.

For the next stage, the designer will attempt to fit furniture to the zoning layout. One of the easiest practical ways to do this is to use templates (scale representations of the furniture), which can easily be moved about the plan to try out planning options. Reference should be made to ergonomic requirements and the design principles. As soon as viable planning solutions begin to emerge, the designer will need to consider the three-dimensional implications of the two-dimensional plan by making simple drawings (sketch elevations, sketch axonometric, isometric views or sketch perspectives) using the proposed furniture layout. Despite being sketches, if they are carefully drawn they will give a strong indication of the effectiveness of the proposed design. Decisions can begin to be made about the balance of the composition and if necessary adjustments can be made to improve aesthetic or practical aspects of the work.

It is probable that initial selections of furniture that work with the overall style of the project will already have been made by this stage, and the dimensions of these pieces should be reflected in the planning options considered. However, it is vital that the designer remains flexible throughout the planning process; it may be necessary to source new pieces of furniture if the planning shows that the original selections are inappropriate in terms of size. Revisions to the plan during space planning do not indicate any failure on the part of the designer; rather they show that the process is working as it should to produce the best possible solution. It is important to ensure that the balance between practical and aesthetic is carefully considered, as planning naturally tends toward the practical, sometimes at the expense of good aesthetics. The evolving design should be continually questioned and, where necessary, any problems should be resolved by further planning and visualization.

Inclusive design

—

It is human nature to imagine that, to a large degree, the abilities (and therefore the experiences) of others closely mirror our own. If we have no difficulty getting around in our day-to-day use of buildings, then we expect that others will have a similar encounter with the buildings that they use. Given a little thought, it should be obvious that many people will actually have a very different experience of a building to ours. Not to consider their needs means that we potentially exclude them from the spaces that we design, which is not a moral (or legal) position that designers can justify. Inclusive design tries to understand the needs of all potential users of a space and to provide for these needs. It ensures that people are put at the center of the design process and responds to human diversity in a positive way. It provides the individual, whatever their abilities, with freedom, dignity, and choice about the way they live their lives, and it delivers spaces that retain flexibility of use.

The range of people who might experience problems using buildings is wider than many would appreciate. It does, of course, include those with disabilities (accounting for almost 20% of the population), but it also includes senior citizens, parents with young children, and people carrying heavy or awkward items. All these groups may have difficulty in negotiating entrances or navigating spaces that ambulant people take for granted. Visual or hearing impairments and learning difficulties cause problems for some, while others face problems because of a lack of manual dexterity.

Addressing these issues may be achieved through research into the problems and solutions available, or it might be appropriate to use access consultants or other specialists who can advise on the practical measures that should be considered.

Good inclusive design will make the planning solutions that are developed better for everyone, and it will always make sense to build inclusive solutions into a design from the very beginning of a project rather than retrospectively. When aiming for the highest standards in all aspects of design, it can be challenging to find aesthetically rewarding solutions to some issues. There is, however, a great deal of scope for developing bespoke solutions in some situations. Manufacturers of kitchen and bathroom equipment are beginning to see the opportunities for incorporating inclusive solutions into their designs, but it is still incumbent on the designer to consider the potential issues and provide fully resolved designs that meet the needs of a diverse population.

5.18a

5.18b

5.18a–15.8b

Accessible design does not need to be brash or visually clumsy to meet
the needs of all users. The form and positioning of this reception desk at
the Museum of London means that wheelchair users have easy access to
the low-level reception desk. It is also brightly lit meaning that it is easy
to identify for those with visual impairments, and that users of the space
who are hearing impaired should be able to lip-read staff more easily.

Case study: **The Old Bengal Warehouse, UK**

Conran and Partners were engaged by restaurant owners and operators D&D to develop a design solution for The Old Bengal Warehouse, a 300-year-old building in London, UK. For much of its working life, the building was used to store many exotic imports and prime among these were spices, cigars, mother of pearl, and wine.

The warehouse space available for development consisted of several spaces with limited circulation between them, though each of the four major spaces could be accessed from the same street frontage.

After initial research on the history and potential of the building, one of the first decisions that had to be made was whether to treat the building as four separate units linked only by their common history and location, or whether to unite the four spaces under one overarching concept.

The concept design presented to, and ultimately agreed to by, the client proposed four discrete units, each one focusing on a unique food and beverage offer aimed at a unique customer demographic. Each unit would adopt one of the major imports (spices, cigars, mother of pearl, and wine) to drive the aesthetic and material considerations of the space. The units were resolved in the following way:

→ A bar with indoor and covered outdoor seating. Spices are the concept adopted for this space.

→ A fine-dining steak restaurant. The rich luxury of cigars defines the feel of this unit.

→ An informal fish restaurant. The natural maritime connection with mother of pearl gives creative direction here.

→ A wine shop with a limited food and drink offering. Traditional wine crates offer a simple but effective link to the concept.

Through materials and color, the designs for each space allude to their concept but still allow the history and construction of the building to show through, with original features such as cast iron columns and brick kept visible.

5.19

5.19

Concept images for the fish restaurant evoke an appropriate atmosphere.

5.20

5.20

A computer-generated rendering of the proposed design helps to communicate the proposal.

5.21

5.21

The completed restaurant: note the similarities and the differences against the visual.

Interview: Conran & Partners

Tina Norden, associate director at Conran & Partners discusses hospitality design, which includes sites such as restaurants, hotels, spas, bars, and nightclubs. Good organization of the space is critical to successful hospitality design.

What do you find challenging and interesting about hospitality design?

→ I love the fact that it's design for enjoyment, for people's relaxation and pleasure. Hospitality projects allow for creativity and imagination whilst also being intensely challenging, as everything needs to run like clockwork in a hotel or restaurant and that requires all parties, from designer to operator and everyone in between, to work closely.

Are there issues in hospitality design that set it apart from other areas of interior design?

→ Hospitality projects tend to have a quick turnaround. One key item they all share is that functionality is a huge part of a successful design. Whether flow of service, wide enough corridors, back-of-house delivery routes, or simply space between chairs—if the function is not right then the project does not work.

Our initial experience of a space is usually driven by the visual impression it makes. In hospitality design, how important are other sensory aspects?

→ A noisy, buzzy space says something very different to a hushed, calm, and quiet ambience. Getting this right for the concept is key. We always end up with debates over the type of music played as this makes a huge difference to the guest experience.

Hospitality design sometimes requires spaces to be multifunctional. How do you reconcile the need for flexibility while still producing interesting interiors?

→ Hospitality design is intrinsically multifunctional but some areas, in particular lobbies and function rooms, really do need to work for a multitude of uses. Design is best when it can be tailored and specific, but if it has to be all things to all people it is more difficult to create personality.

Is it possible for hospitality design to be both luxurious and sustainable?

→ Luxury and sustainability are not opposites, a sustainable approach is possible for any project—it simply comes down to the aspirations and attitude of client and design team.

How do you see hospitality design developing?

→ People are much more design-educated today and recognize good design whether it is a budget hotel or a five-star resort. It is also important to keep moving with the zeitgeist and keeping up to date, being aware of industry trends, and looking at each project afresh. The challenge is to achieve all of this on ever-tighter budgets!

5.22

Careful choice of materials and furnishings allows this hotel to reach a very high standard of environmental performance. One of the suites is illustrated here.

5.22

Activity

—

01. While visiting a large public space (e.g. a museum or a restaurant):

→ Look for evidence of any ordering systems within the space. If they are evident, ask yourself if you would have applied them in a similar manner to the design. If they are not present, can you suggest ways in which they could have been used to enhance the experience of the space? You could try sketching some suggestions.

→ Observe how people react to the space, and how they interact with each other. Does the design make interaction between individuals easy and comfortable? What steps has the designer taken to enable this aspect of the design to work. Is the design inclusive?

02. After your visit to a large public space, consider a much smaller residential space with which you are familiar.

→ Do you think it is easier or more difficult to apply ideas, such as ordering systems, to this space?

→ Is it easier or more difficult to make the design inclusive?

The Human Interface

In earlier chapters, we have looked at the creation of a successful three-dimensional design for a space. What we have not looked at so far is the decorative scheme. The term is actually slightly misleading; the dictionary definition of the word "decorative" suggests that decoration by itself is shallow and vacuous, with no useful purpose. In interior design this is not so, as it is the decorative scheme that adds those elements that complete the sensory experience. Interior design gives purpose to decoration. It adds texture, light, and color. It can help bind the different elements of a design together, or it can introduce interest through variety. The selection of furniture, finishes, fabrics, and hard materials is another major opportunity for you to make your mark on the project.

This chapter looks at the different aspects of the decorative side of interior design and focuses on the user's experience of the space—particularly the way that sight, touch, and sound define that experience as the prime communicators of the designed environment—the interface between the user and the space.

6.1

6.1

The use of a limited palette of materials enhances the overall space in this modern living room and allows the light and textural qualities to provide focus and interest. The simple geometry together with bold-shaped furniture enclose and divide the space.

Materials and finishes

—

Every single part of an interior has a job to do and it needs to be fit for purpose, but each part also has aesthetic properties as well as practical ones. The practical considerations may well define our choices to a great degree, but there will usually still be some flexibility in that choice, and this is where our imagination and creativity can be used to good effect, particularly with regard to our choice of surface treatment.

Selecting materials

—

What is so special about materials and finishes? Why do some designers find the search for new and innovative materials such an exciting part of the job? It is because materials have the unique ability to help us connect at an elemental level through touch and sight with the intent and soul of a project. The look or feel of a material can communicate mood and emotion in a very special way. Natural materials (wood and stone, for example) suggest a certain quality and honesty about the design, whether or not the materials are expensive. In addition to this emotional response to materials, the designer needs to consider the practical aspects of the material choice, but this is another instance where it is the designer's responsibility to find the balance between practicality and aesthetics.

Precisely which materials should be chosen will be guided very much by the feeling that the designer wants to create, and it is the concept that will provide the lead for this.

When working through the practical needs of the design solution, it is unlikely that you will find that there is just one single material that will be suitable. There may well be two or three materials that could be used equally successfully, so you have the opportunity to work through the different options and decide which material will create the best aesthetic impression.

A diverse but harmonious selection of materials that beautifully express their natural features provides a richness to the scheme that in some cases obviates the need for superfluous decoration. Honest materials that are simply expressed are a delight to see and touch. These qualities may not be readily apparent in the planning stages of a project, but they should be considered as early as possible if their impact is to be maximized.

6.2

6.2

The reflective surface
and depth of color
create a mysterious
and intriguing feel to
this table by Based
Upon. The handcrafted
feel of the piece
adds to its allure.

Core materials

—

While a countless number of individual materials could be specified, the core categories of hard materials to be considered for their decorative as well as practical properties are stone, wood, metal, and glass. Designers should consult with suppliers before specifying materials to ensure they are fit for purpose. Suppliers can also advise how materials can be shaped, fixed, and finished.

Stone

Stone provides a real connection to "earth" and has an open, honest quality. Often, limestone, slate, granite, and marble are the first choices of stone, but even within these basic forms the variety is infinite. Different surface finishes provided by the supplier can show off the natural pattern to great advantage, and they may also have practical properties (slip resistance, for example) that should be considered before specifying.

6.3

Specialist finishes add a distinctive feel to an interior scheme by Based Upon. Commissioning pieces from craftspeople allows the designer to inject a unique element into a scheme.

6.4

This metallic surface has pattern and texture. Materials such as this can be used in many applications, for example as surface decoration and applied to walls.

6.3

6.4

Wood

Wood is another elemental material that connects us to nature. Broadly speaking, wood may be supplied as solid timber cut straight from a felled tree, or it may be in the form of timber products, such as plywood and MDF (medium density fiberboard), where the raw timber has undergone some form of processing. Timber products (sometimes called "panel products") can have many different surface treatments applied (real wood veneers, spray paint, powder coating), but their use can feel "cheap" and dishonest to some clients. Wood has a warmth and beauty that is quite unique.

6.5

Beautiful and simply expressed materials are powerful tools for the designer and can evoke all sorts of responses in the viewer. Here, the rosewood face of a peninsular kitchen unit meets the terrazzo floor. A small separation between the two materials allows the inclusion of concealed lights, making the unit appear to float over the floor.

6.6

Architectural metal mesh is a relatively new material that has many decorative and practical possibilities. The meshes come in different weave patterns, and many can be wrapped around a structure or suitable framework.

6.5

6.6

125

Metal

Metal finishes can be supremely practical in some situations and they can also be very decorative. Different types of metal have different visual qualities that the designer can exploit. It gives an interior a sense of modernity, strength, and usually also a masculine edge. Some surface finishes are not as durable as might be imagined, so careful selection is needed. Fabrication of some items can also prove costly and time-consuming, and it pays to work closely with the people that know this material well from the outset.

Glass

As long as the proper precautions are taken, there is no need to fear the use of glass in interiors. It can be costly, but technology allows for the use of glass as semi-structural elements, which can look stunning and provide the perfect foil to other materials specified within a scheme. Again, the designer must make use of the technical expertise of the supplier.

6.7

6.7

Concrete, usually considered a utilitarian and coarse material, is made delicate by this lace-patterned surface on precast concrete. Any discord between our expectations of a material and the reality that we come across peaks our interest and fascination with the material. Concrete is a material with lots of possibilities that can be used in various interior applications.

6.8

6.8

The lower floor of this London restaurant is
intended for private functions; hence, it is more
moody and intimate than the floor above. The brass
screen on the staircase picks up the flickering
flame of the mirror-framed fireplace that is the
focal point of the room. This is a good example of
a rich but well-balanced palette of materials.

Textiles

—

Humans have used textiles (materials composed of fibers) in various forms for thousands of years. The majority of textiles are woven, and the earliest evidence of weaving comes from impressions of textiles, basketry, and nets made on pieces of clay that date back 27,000 years, though weaving on a practical scale developed around 5,000 years ago in Egypt.

Within interiors, textiles are generally apparent in the form of soft furnishings and window treatments. Although alternatives to textiles do exist, they are still the obvious choice when a flexible material is required for furniture manufacture or to provide control of light at a window. Their flexibility and pliability mean that they are comfortable and easy to work with. But textiles are not just a practical solution to a need; they introduce a tactile quality that adds another dimension to the palette of materials associated with a decorative scheme.

They can do great things for our senses; they catch and turn light, and they create dramatic shifts of light and shade, introducing rich texture as they hang in folds. Fabric can be used within the scheme to tell a story: shimmering surfaces of crushed velvets stir memories of grass waving in the breeze, while almost invisible sheers tell a story of soft mist on a summer morning. Fabric can be a way of capturing delightful experiences from real life, and it can allow those moments to become a part of the organized composition of an interior scheme. They have a vital part to play in communicating the mood that you want to capture.

For practical purposes, woven textiles (fabrics) are categorized by the origins of the fibers that make the yarn from which they are made:

→ Natural fibers are derived from vegetable and animal sources, and include fabrics such as cotton, linen (from the flax plant), silk, wool, and horsehair. These are fabrics that look and feel quite different to one another, but generally they all resist dirt reasonably well. Their natural origins make them popular with designers.

→ Man-made fibers are manufactured from processed natural sources. Rayon, acetate, and viscose all come from cellulose obtained from wood, although they are all produced using slightly different processes. They were developed to imitate silk, and for this reason they are still in widespread use. Natural silk has several drawbacks and these substitutes perform better in most respects.

→ Synthetic fibers are derived entirely from chemicals, often petrochemicals. Nylon, polyester, and acrylic are all examples of synthetic fibers. Although practical fabrics, they can pick up dirt easily. The manner in which the fibers are woven will control the look of the fabric to a large extent.

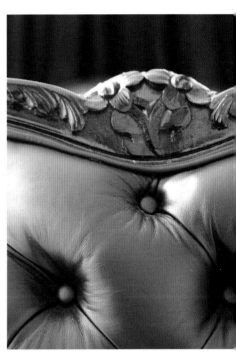

6.9

6.10

6.11

6.9

It is possible to find unusual and interesting textiles that catch the imagination. Using antique textiles can add richness and depth. This gilded leather upholstery can be found in the Winter Hall at Rosenholm Castle in Denmark.

6.10

Textiles can add an interesting dimension to the palette of materials used in a decorative scheme. Here, a contemporary design by Timorous Beasties makes reference to the past and the present. The fabric styles itself after the printed cotton toile de Jouy that originated in France 250 years ago, but the typical bucolic scenes of the original are replaced with urban alternatives.

6.11

Textiles can easily be used to revitalize old pieces of furniture. The carved wooden frame of this chair has been repainted with a silver finish and upholstered with leather that shows an unusual sheen. The form of the chair is traditional, but the materials used have a contemporary edge. Revitalizing old pieces in this way is also a good environmental choice.

Sourcing materials

—

One skill that new designers need to develop is that of sourcing. Essentially, sourcing is searching for the right supplier to provide the materials or products that you need, but there is more to the task than first meets the eye. One issue is that of exclusivity; that is, finding materials that are new and inspirational for the client. This will generally mean looking at specialist suppliers that are geared to dealing largely with designers and architects, rather than the general public. It doesn't necessarily follow that exclusive must be expensive, but this will often be the case. For projects with smaller budgets, the designer may need to be ingenious in their sourcing and use of materials if the feeling of exclusivity is to be maintained, but it is still possible to create memorable interiors.

Sourcing with a purpose—that is with a definite idea in mind about what it is that is required—will make sourcing expeditions efficient. It is still good practice to keep your mind open for the unexpected find, though. Try to think how it might be possible to introduce unusual materials or common materials used for uncommon applications.

Sourcing begins with the concept. Ask yourself: "What ideas am I trying to communicate? What materials reinforce those ideas?" For a city loft that is meant to mirror the professional and sophisticated outlook of the owner, brushed or polished metal, glass, and leather might all be appropriate. In a home that is intended to provide a sanctuary from the bustle of the outside world, sheer fabric, mother of pearl, and unfinished timber could all be good choices.

When looking for materials rather than specific items of furniture, it is possible to source in a manner that supports the concept without actually knowing at the time of sourcing where the sourced materials will be used within the decorative scheme. Once a selection of materials is assembled, it can be edited, and the materials assigned to different tasks within the scheme, all the while making sure that practical considerations are being taken into account. For example, looking back at the previous example, the brushed metal finish that would be so appropriate in our city loft could be added as a bespoke treatment to a tabletop, or to shelving, or it could be used more daringly as wall cladding or flooring.

Timescales during projects can be short, so it will help to be continually on the lookout for new and interesting ideas that could be used at some future date. While many designers now source via the Internet, there is still something to be said for the practice of maintaining a product library in the form of printed brochures, information, and samples that are categorized and filed away for reference. The product knowledge gained by looking at magazines and requesting information from manufacturers and suppliers will equip the designer with an easy source of ideas for use in projects.

6.12

6.12

Careful sourcing of furniture and materials
can create an eye-catching composition. In
this example from Based Upon, the design
on the wall moldings is echoed in the texture
on the head of the classical sculpture, while
the sleek, modern table contrasts with these
elements to achieve a contemporary twist.

The decorative scheme

—

If sourcing is the search for raw materials, then the compilation of the decorative scheme is the means by which all the raw materials are brought together in consort for the final performance.

When creating a decorative scheme, the novice designer will usually direct their first thoughts toward color. It is, of course, a vital aspect of any scheme, but it is only a part. In fact, there are three main components (or properties) of a scheme: texture, form, and color. So what is a successful scheme about? It has a job to do; in addition to providing a comfortable environment for us to inhabit, the scheme is the vehicle by which the original interpretation of mood that came from the design analysis and concept are carried into the real world. How well that mood is interpreted will depend on how well the three properties have been blended in the final scheme.

Part of the task that a designer faces is the need to explore ways of introducing all three components. If a successful scheme is a reflection of the designer's original concept, then returning to that concept will provide clues as to how texture, form, and color can work together to convey mood. When discussing the use of concepts in Chapter 2, it was suggested that abstract interpretations of the ideas of form, texture, color, style, and mood expressed in the brief were the best way to construct a concept. This gives the designer real freedom to find interesting materials or furnishings that pick up on these references, or even to create solutions of their own by commissioning bespoke items.

6.13

6.13

Small decorative touches, such as the glass pieces that hang from this central light, all have their part to play in the larger scheme. Here, they reflect the color from the concealed lighting and add warmth to the room. It is important to determine if the decorative scheme is deficient in any way by looking at the combination of finishes together on a sample board or similar, then adding color, texture, or form as appropriate. Compare the palette of materials with the concept to ensure compatibility.

← Materials and finishes
↓ **The decorative scheme**
→ Acoustics

06

Texture

—

Of the three elements, texture is the one that is most often overlooked, but it is vital in providing visual and tactile interest as it supports the other elements in communicating the feelings generated by the concept. In this context, the word texture is used in its broadest sense: it covers properties such as solidity, reflectivity, translucency, and transparency, as well as the physical surface texture or form of a material. Patterns within a material are often allied to the innate texture, though this relationship is sometimes modified if finishing processes (polishing or sanding, for example) are carried out. Texture is often about light, or what the material does with light. Does it create shadow and highlight? Does it filter the light and modify it in some way?

Texture can be found in all manner of guises; it can be the roughness of a piece of chenille fabric or the natural undulations of unfinished timber. It could be the luster of brushed steel or the combination of reflectivity and transparency captured by a sheet of glass. Texture by itself is not enough, though; it is the variety of texture across different materials that is so important in stimulating interest in a scheme.

Monotony of texture will produce a scheme that looks and feels bland, uninspiring, and ultimately unsatisfactory, even when there is variation in color. Many assume minimalist schemes to contain no color (other than white) or texture, but this is far from the truth. Truly minimalist interiors, such as the Barcelona Pavilion by Mies van der Rohe or the Nový Dvůr Monastery by John Pawson, show restraint in the palette of materials used but a real diversity in the texture of the materials.

To prove to yourself just how important texture is, look carefully at some illustrations of interiors and assess the impact of texture. When you find an illustration of an interior that you particularly like, ask yourself how the major instances of texture are expressed within the scheme and what you would feel about the interior if the variety of texture was not present.

6.14

Texture is vital to providing visual and tactile interest. This textured sideboard creates a focal point with its mix of unusual materials; the smooth sides contrast strongly with the fluted metallic panels.

6.14

Form (or shape)

—

Form is probably the most obvious indicator of a particular style within a scheme. Furniture declares the period from which it originates through its shape and other cues of pattern and surface decoration. For example, the art nouveau style, which made its presence felt at the end of the nineteenth and start of the twentieth century, was characterized by organic, curvilinear shapes that are readily identified with that period even today. In contrast, the prevalent style throughout the 1920s and 1930s, now known as art deco, expressed the style of the times through regular, geometric shapes and faceted three-dimensional forms. Popular motifs were the starburst and the ziggurat. Anyone wishing to recreate the period look within an interior must take note of the dominant forms of a particular style. Even when it is not the intention to overtly copy or recreate a particular period, use of distinctive shapes, motifs, glyphs, and typefaces can all suggest a link to a previous era.

Pattern needs careful handling by the designer to ensure success. It is necessary to visualize how the pattern will appear in the finished space, paying particular attention to the scale of the pattern. Pattern that seems attractive and appropriate when looking at a small sample may be lost when applied to large surfaces. Conversely, large pattern can seem overwhelming and inappropriate when viewing small samples, but when seen in situ, those problems can disappear. The designer should use drawing or other visualization techniques to ensure a good understanding of the likely effects of pattern before specifying.

6.15

6.15

Here, form and pattern are used to strengthen the design scheme. The strong lines exhibited in the overhead light are echoed in the draped curtains, the decorative wallpaper, and the shape of the rug. The minimalist seating supplies restraint and creates harmony within the overall scheme.

← Materials and finishes
↓ **The decorative scheme**
→ Acoustics

06

Thinking point: Constructing a scheme

—

The use of sample boards as presentation tools is detailed in the following chapter, but the process of constructing a scheme will follow the pattern outlined here.

Firstly, collect as many sample materials as possible from suppliers. These should all connect with the concept in some way; color should come from the palette suggested by the concept, and texture and form should also work in sympathy with the visual references suggested by the concept. At this stage, fabrics and hard materials do not necessarily have to be sourced for specific functions; it is more important that the designer has a generous number of options to choose from. Suppliers who are used to working with professional designers and architects will usually be happy to provide their clients with free samples that are ideal for sample boards.

Try to represent all the surfaces and finishes that will be present. Pieces of board can be painted up using sample paints and even when specifying bespoke items, it is usually possible to obtain samples from the manufacturer. If, despite all efforts, it is not possible to get physical samples, then photographs can be used. Photos are also helpful when showing materials that have large pattern repeats, which might not be fully represented on the samples obtained. Ideally, they should be used in conjunction with the physical sample, rather than instead of it.

Clear a workspace so that it is possible to see the emerging scheme away from any distracting influences; begin to assign materials to specific positions or functions within the scheme, making sure that they are suitable for the intended purpose.

If there is more than one possibility, try each material in place and assess its success in combination with the other materials. As this process continues, some of the options will begin to appear as favorites, while others will edit themselves out of the scheme, simply because they do not work as well as others. These samples should not be discarded, though, because as the scheme develops and new relationships are established between the finishes, the emphasis in color, form, or texture can shift, and materials that once were cast aside could find a use again.

Arrange all the selected materials in a composition that roughly reflects their logical place within the space—flooring at the bottom of the grouping, ceiling finish at the top, and materials that would be adjacent to one another in the finished scheme placed in a similar relationship in the composition. In order to appreciate the effectiveness of the scheme as fully as possible, it is important to mimic the proportions of each finish relative to the others. This can be achieved simply by folding and taping fabrics or wallpapers, and by masking hard materials. If materials are not shown in proportion, the sample scheme is likely to look radically different to the installed scheme. Include all ancillary finishes (for example, paint colors for architraves, windowsills, and frames) or, once again, there is a risk that the look of the sample board will be distorted.

From this point, it is possible to make an informed judgment as to the success of the scheme and, if necessary, make changes before any money has been committed to purchases. Working with sample schemes gives the designer the chance to experiment and still be fairly confident of the result.

The power of color

—

Color is discussed later in this chapter, but it should be noted here that the power of color within the decorative scheme is enormous. It is a great indicator of mood, and our response to color is experienced on a very elemental level. Often, though, color is one area that individuals feel most insecure about. The worry can be that the client will reject the color choices of the designer, and students often feel reluctant to impose their view of color upon the client. Once again, the concept should be allowed to serve as the source of our color choices. When a good deal of effort has been expended in evaluating the desires of the client and interpreting them visually in the concept, it should be possible to let that concept dictate the color scheme, using not only the colors but bearing in mind the proportions, too. If these aspects of the concept are followed faithfully, along with ideas of texture and form, then it is almost certain that the finished scheme will capture and communicate the original intent of the concept.

Putting the scheme together

—

Finding colors, styles, and textures that work with the concept may be the starting point, but the designer also needs techniques for assembling the scheme and checking that it is creating the desired effect.

Yet again, sketching is likely to play a part at this stage of the development of the design. Perspective sketches or elevations of the space can be rendered as simply or elaborately as desired in order to assess the impact of color choices. However, this alone will not be adequate to evaluate the subtleties of the ways in which different materials play off one another, and the nuances of other effects such as texture and reflectivity. The best way to do this is to create a facsimile of the scheme using the actual materials that are being proposed on sample boards. Sample boards are used to explain schemes to clients, but they are also extremely important during the initial design stages because they provide the palette upon which the finished scheme is mixed and refined.

6.16

A largely muted color scheme is dramatically lifted by the use of a strong accent color and variety in texture and reflectivity of surfaces.

← Materials and finishes
↓ **The decorative scheme**
→ Acoustics

06

6.16

Acoustics

—

Our brains use more than the senses of sight and touch to form their understanding of the environment that surrounds us, and one of the prime sensations that we experience and that becomes part of our response to our surroundings is that of sound. In the same way that a film soundtrack is as important to our understanding of that film as the visuals, so our everyday lives are informed to a large degree by what we hear and how sound is modified by the local environment.

Imagine walking between the dense, close-growing trunks of fir trees in the forests of northern Europe or North America. The feeling of stillness and oppressive closeness of the surroundings is amplified by the muffled quality of the sounds reaching our ears. Not only is there an absence of loud noise because of the blanket of trees and the carpet of pine needles, but any sound that does reach us is flat and dead because of the acoustic qualities of the forest floor and the bark of the trees; irregular surfaces absorb the sound energy so that we only hear the sound that reaches us directly, with little echo or reverberation. In this way, the sights and sounds of a location work in tandem to create our instinctive reaction to the place. By way of contrast, an indoor swimming pool will probably generate a very different response from us. Even without other people present, the sound of any movement that we make is augmented by scores of echoes, which combine to create a strident clamor, bright and brassy in nature. Add in the presence of other people, and the effect is magnified. People raise their voices, making still more noise, in an escalating battle to be heard.

Acoustic experiences

—

The way that sound is experienced can add to or detract from our perception and experience of place, and as designers we have the tools to modify and control the acoustic properties of an interior. Opportunities exist to modify either the surface finish or form of a material in order to change its acoustic qualities, and we might also be able to influence the construction techniques used. Designers should be aware of the ways in which this can be done and should be prepared to make use of them, or to seek assistance, where appropriate to ensure that this important aspect of our experience of the space is not overlooked.

Where the acoustic properties of a space are critical to its function, it would be sensible to employ the services of an acoustic engineer. If necessary, the space can be surveyed in detail; dedicated software applications can be used to judge the acoustic performance of the space, and appropriate measures can be taken. This is most definitely the science part of acoustics. For a less critical application (which is likely to mean the vast majority of commissions that the designer is asked to work on), a good working knowledge of the properties of materials and the basic physics of acoustics should be adequate. This is where the control of the acoustic is more art than science, and it is well within the ability of the interior designer to manage this.

We hear sound as a result of sound energy that is transmitted as a series of vibrations. These vibrations are able to travel through air and through the various materials that we use to build and furnish the spaces that we live and work in. However, these materials do not all conduct sound energy to the same degree; through careful selection of materials, we can reduce the impact of transmitted sound or modify its quality so that a more appropriate result is obtained.

6.17

6.17

Generous window treatments not only allow for easy control of light and privacy; they also make excellent attenuators of unwanted sound in this city apartment. Even during the day, the large areas of fabric that cover the walls help to deaden sound from passing traffic.

Controlling acoustics

—

Controlling the acoustic qualities of an interior might involve one or more of the following:

→ Preventing or reducing unwanted sound from entering the space.

→ Preventing or reducing sound generated within the space from reaching other areas of a building or the local neighborhood.

→ Planning space so that functions that are acoustically incompatible are separated.

→ Changing the quality of sound heard within a space in order to modify the user experience.

Sound that is either leaking into or out of a building can be dealt with by ensuring that windows and doors are fitted well. Windows can be upgraded to either double- or triple-glazed units, if appropriate, and simple measures—such as draft excluders—may help to a degree. If existing doors are to be retained, a carpenter should make sure that they fit as closely as possible to the doorframe. If doors can be replaced, then upgrading the construction may help; solid hardwood doors perform more efficiently than other materials with regard to sound insulation.

The methods used in wall, floor, and ceiling construction also play their part in the transmission of sound energy. Although the technicalities can be quite complicated, in essence, lightweight construction methods (such as stud partition walls) will not provide much resistance to the passage of sound, while more rigid constructions (such as

cinder block or breeze block) will absorb the sound energy to a greater degree. If construction using concrete blocks is not appropriate, then it is possible to introduce wall construction of reasonable acoustic performance by ensuring that the space between the outer surfaces is filled with mineral fiber insulation or a similar material. Though primarily used for thermal insulation purposes, these materials will also improve the acoustic performance of the wall. Employing methods of discontinuous construction will also benefit the acoustics. Here, the typical studwork that forms the framing of the wall, which provides a direct link from one face of a wall to the other, is replaced by smaller timbers that do not bridge the gap from one face to the next. Thus, they remove the direct path by which sound can be transmitted between spaces. The addition of a sound-absorbing material, such as sheep's wool insulation or mineral wool, will reduce the transmission of sound still further.

While the preceding methods of acoustic control are practical, they do not allow much aesthetic consideration to be applied to the space. This only really happens when looking at interior surfaces and, as we have seen, there are two traits of the surface that designers can play with to produce the results that they want: surface texture and form. If echoes and reverberation occur when sound waves are repeatedly reflected between parallel surfaces, it follows that if the surfaces can be made nonparallel and nonreflective, then the reverberation or echo will be removed, or at least reduced. This can be achieved in one of three ways:

→ Changing the orientation of one or more of the surfaces such that they do not lie parallel to one another, thus preventing the sound waves from being repeatedly reflected.

→ Changing the shape of a surface such that it is no longer flat (and therefore no longer able to easily reflect sound to another surface). Changes to shape could be large scale: surfaces that are convex (curved outward) will disperse and diffuse the sound waves, while surfaces that are concave (bowed inward) will focus them (sometimes, this effect will be one to be avoided). Changes to shape could also be on a small scale: for example, a multifaceted surface (such as timber slats) will serve to break up sound waves.

→ Changing or adapting the material to alter its acoustic properties. Materials that are hard, such as ceramic tiles, will reflect sound much more readily than those that are soft or resilient such as fabric. Where it is simply not feasible to substitute one material for another, it may be possible to introduce additional materials (for example, fabric hanging in front of a wall or below a ceiling) that will act to absorb sound energy and so modify the acoustic performance of a space. This will, of course, have implications for the decorative scheme, so it needs to be considered in relation to the other materials already existing within the scheme.

6.18

6.18

These decorative plaster tiles by Robin Ellis Design for Butcher Plasterworks, seen here in a restaurant designed by Claire Nelson, create a nonuniform surface that has positive acoustic qualities, as well as great decorative potential. The elimination of hard, flat surfaces helps reduce the reflection of unwanted sound waves.

Furniture

—

The design analysis undertaken at the beginning of a project should have identified the functions that the space needs to accommodate. With those functions in mind, furniture can be selected to fulfill the needs of the brief. But how should furniture be chosen? The answer once again lies in the concept.

Let the concept be the guide when it comes to determining the style of the furniture. Ideas of both form and finish can be extracted from it, and sourcing for the furniture will then have direction and purpose. Having a clear idea of the basic look of a piece of furniture helps immensely as it is necessary to narrow the field to avoid being overwhelmed by choices. That said, it is also important to keep an open mind when sourcing. It is all too easy to miss a piece that would lift a scheme above the ordinary simply because of a fixed idea of what is required.

Furniture items may be designed as individual pieces or they may form part of a larger collection. Pieces from a collection share common style traits, and it could naturally be assumed that sourcing such furniture will provide a strong visual solution. This is sometimes true, but generally only in spaces that work well with some dominant visual characteristics. It is usually best practice to work with furniture from different sources. The differences and individual personalities of several pieces sourced in this way will create a harmonious group that is relaxed, but that still conveys a strong sense of style. When designing with pieces that form a collection, the risk is that the overall look will appear contrived and somewhat unsophisticated. This is another of the judgments that new designers will need to make for themselves, as each situation will have to be judged on its own merits.

6.19

6.19

Unusual pieces of furniture, such as these seats, can provide real interest within a scheme. These pieces are made of resin and finished to a high standard. The hard reflective surfaces and depth of color catch the eye and are ever changing.

6.20

6.20

In this restaurant and bar, furniture has been
built to fit the space. The red banquettes look
comfortable, and the warm color adds to the
effect. The curved seating area and tables fill
the central space, which allows this area to be
used commercially. In restaurant interiors, it
is important to ensure that there is adequate
seating to allow the business to work financially.

Freestanding and built-in furniture

—

Furniture can be categorized as either freestanding or built-in. Freestanding furniture is the most common. It is easy to place within a room, and it is flexible as it can be repositioned at will. However, it is not necessarily the most efficient in terms of use of space. Take, for example, a bookcase sited within an alcove. However carefully sourced to fit, a freestanding bookcase is unlikely to fill exactly the space that it occupies, and this means that the use of space is not as efficient as it could be. In this example, a built-in bookcase will fit the space exactly, with no awkward and inefficient gaps around and behind it. Built-in furniture can create a very considered look within a space. It is unique, so each installation will need to be individually designed or, at the very least, standard-sized elements will need to be put together with unique trims to match the size of the space. This is the approach often taken by the major suppliers of built-in furniture, but the whole piece can be a unique creation, and it can be the designer who is responsible for creating the piece. Some designers will have a thorough knowledge of cabinet construction methods and so retain creative control over every detail of the piece, while others will work with cabinet makers and delegate responsibility for the technicalities of construction, maintaining overall control of the look of the piece. Bespoke pieces of furniture allow for real freedom of expression within the design.

There is no reason why freestanding pieces should not also be commissioned especially for a scheme, if budget permits. Although probably more costly than furniture sourced from stock, within residential projects, bespoke items will usually acquire the status of a family heirloom, and their individuality can provide a compelling reason for a client to agree to their manufacture. The designing and making of bespoke pieces is not to be undertaken lightly, but the furniture that results can be a very special answer to a need. As the car designer Ferdinand Porsche said, "In the beginning, I looked around and could not find the car that I dreamed of. So I decided to build it myself."

6.21

6.21

Freestanding furniture is easy to place in a room
and is much more flexible than built-in furniture. The
simplicity of this chest of drawers by e15 allows the
natural beauty of the wood to make its presence felt.

Color

—

Color is the brain's interpretation of the different wavelengths of visible light waves. The study of color and our everyday experience of it is a mix of both art and science. Scientists, artists, and philosophers have proposed different "color models" as they try to explain how colors work. These models look at attributes of the color, such as hue (the actual color of something), saturation (how pure the color is versus how gray it is), and brightness (how much white or black is a part of the color). Using these parameters, most colors can be described.

A helpful tool for considering the relationship between colors is the color wheel. It takes the linear spectrum seen when light is refracted through a prism and joins the free ends to create a circle. Although this means that colors from opposite ends of the spectrum (red and violet) are now adjacent on the wheel, the effect is a seamless progression of colors from any one point on the wheel to any other point. While one color model may be based on different assumptions about its primary colors to the next model, most are consistent in their placement of color around the wheel. The wheel allows us to visualize and define color harmonies—collections of colors that work together to create a usable scheme. Neutral colors can be important for decorative schemes. True neutrals are black, white, and grays, but in decorative terms the word "neutral" has expanded its meaning to include desaturated and less bright colors, particularly those with an earthy feel.

Research shows that colors can affect the way we feel. The effects are measurable under controlled conditions but often do not manifest themselves to the same degree in real-life situations. The research deals in generalizations, where colors may be described only in broad terms, and the impact or modifying effect of adjacent colors is ignored. Reaction to color is often also a function of cultural and personal experience. It is sensible for designers to be aware of the symbolism of color and use it where appropriate, but remember that it is only one part of a larger whole; context is all.

6.22

When working with color, the designer must look at the overall color scheme. In the lobby of the Avalon Building in New York, designed by Slade Architecture, the color of the seating blends with the rug, while the yellow accent color on the back wall adds contrast and interest. The tones used in the table, walls, and flooring are similar and create a harmonious whole.

6.22

Color schemes

—

We have seen that a visual concept can be used to dictate the color scheme. This allows color schemes to be derived from the brief, but there are other systematic methods of relating colors to form the basis of a scheme. Even when taking a scheme from some other form of inspiration, it may be helpful to determine the type of color scheme being used so that a clear understanding of how the scheme is working can be gained.

The basic types of color scheme are named in relation to how the colors sit on the color wheel. Following a defined structure will usually result in a workable scheme, but flexibility must be allowed. The color wheel should guide rather than dictate. There are so many variables that it does not pay to be dogmatic about the rules of color. For this reason, the schemes as described here should not be seen as exclusive; variations are allowed and desirable. Even in monochromatic schemes, accent colors (small amounts of contrasting color) can lift an otherwise ordinary scheme and transform it into something special. As ever, balance is the key and judgment on these matters is something that needs to be developed.

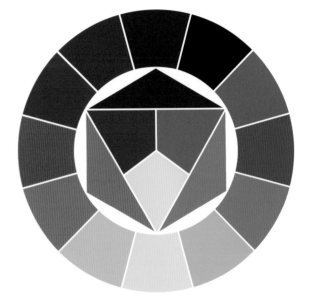

6.23

6.23

The artists' color wheel is an invaluable tool for the designer, offering a guide to workable color combinations and solutions.

Scheme type	Depiction on color wheel	
Monochromatic	Uses different values of a single color.	These schemes can still have large contrasts because of differences in saturation and brightness, or can be differentiated through surface finish for subtle and sophisticated effects such as matte and satin paint. Schemes using neutral colors can be calming and less vibrant, and they need variety of texture and contrast to avoid becoming bland.
Analogous	Uses two or more colors that are adjacent on the color wheel.	These often replicate naturally occurring schemes and are generally calming. Greater contrast between colors will give a stronger result.
Complementary	Colors that are opposite each other on the wheel such as blue and orange, red and green, purple and yellow.	If colors are at full saturation, these schemes are very vibrant. Careful handling of the colors is required to achieve a successful balance.
Split complementary	A scheme with a main color and the two colors on each side of its complementary color on the color wheel.	More subtle than a pure complementary scheme.
Triadic	Any three colors that are equidistant around the color wheel.	Care needs to be taken to achieve balance, though this will be a subjective call.
Tetradic / quadratic	Four colors that have a logical relationship on the color wheel, such as double complementaries.	As triadic (above).

Color perception

—

Our perception of color is influenced by several factors, which means that our experience of color is not absolute; it changes all the time. Some of the reasons why colors seem to shift and change are outlined below:

→ Light sources rarely emit light that is truly white with an even mix of all wavelengths. Incandescent lamps give out relatively warm (red-yellow) light, for example, while other types of artificial light source all have their own color characteristics. Daylight, which is often quoted as a reference standard, will actually change in quality throughout the day, and it is also dependent on geographical location and orientation (the outlook of a space in relation to compass direction).

→ Material surfaces can reflect light in a diffuse or specular (mirrorlike) way.

→ Colors can be changed to a subtly different hue by the presence of other colors nearby.

Because of these and other reasons, it is impossible for us to accurately remember a color. Actual references should always be taken or noted when trying to color match. Reference samples are also helpful when discussing color with clients. If this is tried without specifying exactly what color is being talked about, mistakes will be made—when the client says blue, for example, what blue do you imagine? Is it the same color that the client is imagining?

6.24

6.24

A number of material surface effects are at play in this interior. The richness of the velvet and the faded appearance of the wallpaper in the sunlight combine to create a sense of antiquity and history.

6.25

6.25

A large piece of art provides a major focal point in
this space. The colors employed in the painting
are sympathetic to the rest of the scheme. Which
came first, art or scheme? The presence of nearby
colors can subtly alter the hue of others.

The effects of color on space

—

Color schemes can appear to alter the dimensions of a space. Individual colors can either advance—closing in on the viewer and making spaces feel smaller—or recede and make spaces feel larger. Warm colors (reds, yellows, oranges) and darker tones tend to advance, while cool colors (blues, greens) and lighter tones tend to retreat. These effects can be used to enhance or hide existing features of a space.

Some of the key effects that can be achieved are:

→ Long spaces can be made to feel less like a corridor by using an advancing color on the short walls.

→ Low spaces will feel more spacious with receding colors; high spaces can be lowered with advancing colors.

→ Using similar colors will link and unify multiple spaces.

→ Using receding colors with low contrast between different colors will create a feeling of spaciousness.

→ Strong color contrasts and/or advancing color will reduce the feeling of spaciousness.

Applying color across natural breaks, such as corners, will also alter the feel of a space. It can camouflage the structure and increase the effectiveness of the strategies listed above. For example, to reduce the apparent height of a space, an advancing color can be used on the ceiling and the uppermost section of the walls.

6.26

6.27

6.26

This bathroom utilizes natural finishes and a largely neutral color scheme of gray, brown, black, and white. The red glass acts as an accent color, which lifts the scheme and adds a dynamic quality that would otherwise be missed.

6.27

In this large bedroom in a country house hotel, the dark walls help to hold together the different elements required in the room; the color advances somewhat to give a comfortable feeling of enclosure.

Light

—

Light and color are intimately linked. Both natural light and artificial light play a major role in shaping the decorative scheme. Many projects would benefit from the creative and technical input offered by specialist lighting designers, and if they are to be involved, it is important that they are brought in to the project at the earliest feasible stage. Ideally, this will be before any major planning or design decisions have been made.

If the project is small scale and the interior designer is ready to take on the role of lighting designer, it is still advisable to consider the lighting scheme right from the start rather than as an afterthought. The best effects and schemes are conceived when light is given equal status with the planning of the space. If the project requires the planning and installation of a completely new lighting scheme, then it might be appropriate to allocate as much as 30% of the budget to lighting. That figure may be surprising, but it serves to underline the importance of good lighting to the success of a design proposal.

When designing a lighting scheme, attention should be paid to the proposed colors and finishes, as these have a large bearing on how effective the lighting is.

Natural light

—

Before creating a lighting scheme, the effects of natural light within a space should be understood. How does light travel through the space? How does it vary with time of day and time of year? Would changes to the size, position, or number of windows benefit the scheme? Is the landscape immediately outside the windows responsible for modifying the light that enters the building? Understanding all these points can be difficult when the designer usually only has a very brief period in which they can experience the space for themselves firsthand, but research should be undertaken to allow a complete picture to be built up. Only once that is complete is it possible to decide how artificial light can be added to augment the space.

Artificial light

—

The addition of artificial light allows the designer to put light in specific places for practical need or decorative effect. It can create mood either in isolation or by supplementing natural light. Artificial light is, of course, a necessity if the space is going to function at night. As described earlier when looking at color, each type of light source creates light with different color bias. It is possible to mix different sources, but this needs to be done carefully. Light fittings are likely to evolve radically to cope with the need to reduce energy use over the next few decades.

6.28

This fiber-optic "sky" has been simply installed in the plasterboard ceiling using 144 fiber tails linked to one hidden light source. It is set to illuminate as the main lights are dimmed for film screenings, creating a luxurious home cinema environment.

6.28

155

Lighting schemes

—

Effective lighting schemes create drama and interest by employing light and shade. It is not necessary to flood a space with an even wash of light; in fact, this will lead to bland and uninspiring schemes that are dispiriting. Conversely, the contrast of light and shade is stimulating, and if the user is given adequate control over the lighting scheme, the dramatic use of light can still prove to be practical and effective. The designer should aim to create layers of light by employing different categories of light and light fitting:

→ General or ambient lighting is used to provide an overall level of light that allows us to navigate the space and perform basic noncritical tasks. It is not necessarily uniform in nature, nor does it need to be extremely bright.

→ Accent or feature lighting is used for the purpose of adding detail and interest to the scheme. It may highlight an artwork or an architectural feature, such as an alcove or column.

→ Task lighting provides sufficient illumination for the safe undertaking of specific jobs but can take various forms. It could be a freestanding luminaire for a desk or built-in lighting under kitchen cabinets, for example. It may be a bright but localized light source.

→ Decorative lighting is used primarily as an adjunct to the decorative scheme, its form helping to add the necessary detail and visual interest rather than providing useful illumination.

→ Kinetic lighting includes any light emitted from a flame, such as firelight and candlelight. It is a light source that is randomly variable by nature and gives another layer of interest to the decorative scheme, even if it is somewhat unpredictable.

For a lighting scheme to work well, it must be easily controllable. Adequate and easily accessible switching is the minimum, and it may be desirable to consider automated control and scene-setting controls that create different moods at a single touch. Installation of the light fittings and control equipment can lead to considerable disruption, which emphasizes the need for careful project planning right from the start.

6.29

6.30

6.31

6.29

This lighting scheme reflects the relaxing environment of this newly refurbished Country House Hotel Spa at Barnsley House hotel in the Cotswolds, Gloucestershire, England, while introducing a sense of luxury into the space. The oversized pendant provides an element of dramatic glamor, elongating the space, while the recessed uplighters highlight the organic texture of the local stone behind.

6.30

These modern minimalist stairs use lighting concealed under each step. The effect is to create stairs that appear to float, one above the other, which draw you enticingly on and up the stairs.

6.31

Using downlighters in groups can create an interesting effect. The restaurant Barbecoa in London, UK, uses them in the bar area to create an intimate atmosphere.

Case study: Greene Street Loft, USA

Greene Street is in an area of New York that has a rich heritage of nineteenth-century industrial buildings, many of which have been converted into residential spaces. This project was developed by Slade Architecture as a space where their clients could live, work, and entertain.

The loft was a large open area of some 300 square meters (2950 square feet) bounded on each side by original windows providing light and views. The historic industrial windows were key elements in defining the aesthetic for the loft, and in order to emphasize them the space was kept very open from the front to the back of the building. In order to maximize the spacious feeling, Slade created three large 2.4 meters (8 feet) high rectangular blocks down the center of the loft to define and divide the different areas and living spaces.

The first block consists of a large aluminum bookcase, which holds the owners' collection of Korean trunks and books, and it seeks to separate the main living and entertainment spaces from the client's study. The second block contains a built-in desk area facing the study and a closet on the other side, and the third block contains the other side of the large walk-in closet and the master bathroom.

These freestanding blocks create two slots of spaces that run from the front of the building to the back. These provide a continuous view through the entire depth of the apartment and function as corridors linking the different areas of the apartment.

The full-height laminate wall on the north side of the apartment conceals the storage and utility area, powder room, guest bathroom, services, and a loft sleeping area. Two of the panels create a large pivot door that closes off the bedroom area and provides access to the exit stairs. Each panel of this wall is a different white laminate, all with different finishes and textures—glossy, matte, patterned, textured, metallic, and plain white finishes—although from a distance the wall of these blocks looks like a continuous white surface.

Occupants in this residence experience the space without shoes, so the tactile qualities for the floors were considered in detail. The original wood plank industrial flooring was retained and stained. The bedrooms were raised on a platform of stone textured with fine grooves to accommodate plumbing and radiant floor heating; this also provided a vertical separation for the more private areas in the loft and offered a contrasting floor texture in this zone.

The finished loft is a successful mix of the best of the existing building with a series of considered new spaces that allow for successful family living as well as a generous entertainment space.

6.32

6.33

6.32

The main space in the loft was kept simple and uncluttered to enhance the effect of the existing windows.

6.33

Slade selected all of the furniture and finishes, which included a number of custom-designed items such as a silk rug and a large dining table. The dining table was created from a single slice of Makore timber; it seats 20 people and runs the whole length of the east-facing windows.

Interview: Slade Architecture

Hayes and James Slade are architects who designed the Greene Street loft. Together, they run Slade Architecture in New York, USA.

How did the brief and the design process inform the scheme?

→ Our design approach is unique for each project including our work at Greene Street, but it is framed by a continued exploration of primary architectural concerns. As architects and designers, we operate with intrinsic architectural interests: the relationship between the body and space, movement, scale, time, perception, materiality and its intersection with form.

In this project, the iconic Soho loft was our setting and our clients had specific interests in entertaining in a generous atmosphere, accommodating overnight guests easily, and Asian antiques.

What was your philosophy behind your choice of materials for the project?

→ Materials were selected for visual and tactile qualities. We were working toward an undeniably modern design but using elements that would age successfully. We selected classic modern pieces combined with contemporary pieces.

Our selection of materials is intended to be crisp, clean, and engaging in a subtle way that forces the occupant to reconsider the surroundings. For example, there is a panel wall that spans from the front to the back of the loft that is entirely finished with white laminate. Every single panel is a different white laminate (glossy, matte, textured, and so on). On first viewing the wall, one just recognizes a paneled white wall, but upon closer examination it becomes apparent that each panel is slightly and subtly different.

There are some interesting uses of scale throughout the project. Is this a response to the overall space?

→ The large prismatic loft volume is repeated and scaled down in the intermediate dividers that mark the individual program areas. As mentioned above, keeping these elements freestanding and not running full height has the effect that they read as new blocks introduced within the larger volume. We were intrigued by the scalar opportunities that came with the loft configuration.

Were there any challenges with regards to the materials and construction of the project, such as the details and junctions or integration with the existing fabric? How did you overcome these?

→ The biggest challenge in the detailing was offering the possibility of real privacy in the apartment while maintaining the open flow and visual connection between the main spaces. For example, doors between bedrooms and corridors must be functional and convenient but typically remain hidden; the high-level glass partitions above the master bathroom maintain the clear sight lines throughout the apartment but separate the bathroom from the rest of the space.

These solutions all combine to maintain the feeling and scale of the existing space while creating a contextual interior that meets the client's brief.

6.34

The view from the main bedroom shows how the loft was divided using a series of cube volumes with glazed panels in order to maintain visibility through the overall space.

6.34

Activity

—

01. Choose an interior that you find interesting and engaging, preferably one that you have access to rather than one that you know from illustrations alone. Consider the different elements that make the scheme what it is.

→ Can the color scheme be easily classified according to the descriptions given in this chapter?

→ If the scheme does not easily fit into one of those classifications, does it matter?

02. Consider the textural qualities in the room's design.

→ What tactile qualities do the different materials, both hard and soft, possess?

→ Is there a wide variety of texture present?

→ Would the scheme still work with more or less textural variation?

→ Is pattern present in the scheme? If so, is more than one material patterned?

→ What is the relative scale of the patterns?

→ What effect would varying the scale of the pattern have?

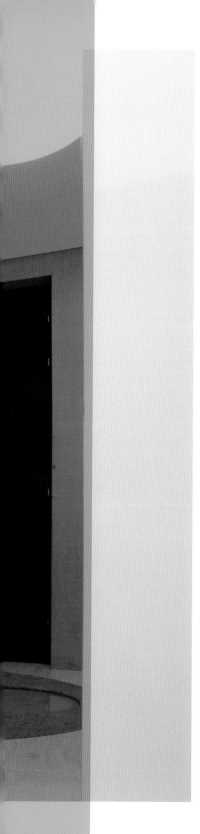

Sustainable Design

Sustainability is a term that most of us have heard but may not fully understand. There is debate over exactly what the term should mean, but one commonly quoted and generally accepted definition defines sustainability as "the ability to provide for our needs without compromising the ability of future generations to provide for their needs."

True as it is, this definition is quite benign and it does not convey the reality of the situation. What we need to understand is that, if we manage to achieve a sustainable society, then over the next couple of centuries or so the planet's resources should be sufficient to continue to support human life here on earth, but if we don't live sustainably, then by definition it will not. So the stakes are high, but what bearing does this have on the everyday work of the interior designer?

A sustainable future will only come about if we change the way we live and make different lifestyle choices. As designers, we can respond to the sustainability agenda in three basic areas:

Material selection: Sources and provenance, embodied energy, process and transport energy.

Conservation: Conservation of resources, efficient design, specification.

Occupier behavior: How people use the space—for example, provision of a shower promotes cycling or running to work. Staircases rather than lifts promote interaction and health.

7.1

7.1

This entrance hall to a sustainable house in Holland does not instantly disclose its sustainability credentials, but it is both stylish and contemporary (see also the case study on page 174).

Why is sustainability an issue?

—

Modern man first left Africa well over 100,000 years ago. Human population gradually increased, in a broadly steady manner, until relatively recently (the last couple of centuries or so) when that rate of increase became exponential. During the twentieth century alone, the planet's population increased threefold from two billion to over six billion.

While our planet was easily able to support the demands of a much smaller and relatively unsophisticated human population in earlier centuries, the developed world today consumes an unsustainable amount of the earth's natural resources. It is only because the majority of the world's human population currently take proportionally less from the planet than the developed minority that serious problems are not yet a part of our day-to-day experience.

However, as the number of countries that are classed as developed grows, and as emerging nations reach higher up the development ladder, that minority of the population (currently around 20%) that take the majority (typically 75%) of resources will increase in number. Studies have shown that as countries become more developed (and more industrialized), damage to the environment increases.

In short, our increasing consumption of the earth's natural resources is not sustainable; we cannot continue to exploit those resources (such as crude oil, which is processed into a huge array of products) at an increasing rate and expect all our wants to be met.

The reason that this is of concern to interior designers is because the construction and day-to-day running of a building consumes a great deal of energy and resources. Through the choices that they make when fitting out or refurbishing a building, designers will have the opportunity to affect, for better or worse, the environment. As designers, our answer to the problem should be that for every project we undertake, we pledge to minimize the impact on the environment of that project through the choices that we make.

Although the subject of sustainability is presented here as a chapter in its own right, designers should understand that thinking about (and acting upon) sustainability issues needs to be an integral part of the design process. They must consider the possibilities for creating lower impact interiors all the way through the project; it must become just as much a part of the job as space planning, accessibility issues, or sourcing, and not just an "add-on" that is considered after everything else.

7.2

7.2

Many designers are unaware of the connection between timber used in construction and furniture production and the effects on the environment when that timber is illegally logged. Rain forests, such as this one in Indonesia, are being destroyed due to illegal logging.

Where choices are made

—

Choices regarding sustainability can be made at the building structure level (when creating new-build structures or when refurbishing existing ones); when deciding on appropriate furniture and fittings for a design proposal, and even in the choices of surface covering and finishes when dealing with a decorative scheme, as described below.

Building construction practices

—

Building technologies of the last few decades have made full use of modern materials. Unfortunately, what drove the development of many of these technologies was performance and speed of construction; sustainability was not an issue. Consequently, many existing structures have been constructed with materials that have poor environmental credentials, and the buildings that they have been used to create were not designed to minimize the consumption of energy in their day-to-day use.

7.3

7.3

Although this is a traditional room, the paint used on the wall is organic and is free of any volatile organic compounds (VOCs). VOCs are thought to contribute to low-level atmospheric pollution. This solvent-free paint is produced by Ecos Organic Paints.

New buildings

—

Materials such as reinforced concrete, for example, are ubiquitous in modern construction, yet the production of reinforced concrete elements of a building, whether in situ or off-site, takes no account of their disposal once the useful life of the building has passed. This means that demolition can be time-consuming, costly, and damaging to the environment, and it can be difficult to reuse or recycle the materials afterward.

Modern construction that does consider sustainability will, first of all, promote the use of materials that have minimal impact on the environment (commensurate with engineering performance), and they will be used to construct buildings which themselves use reduced amounts of energy. Some of the strategies employed to reduce energy use are very simple and in fact refer back to pre-industrial architectural ideas for their inspiration. For example, using greater amounts of insulation will help reduce heat loss when external temperatures are below those of the interior; it also reduces internal heat gain when external temperatures rise. Having opening windows on opposite aspects of a building can promote cross ventilation that can make buildings comfortable when external temperatures are raised. These very simple approaches to making the interior environment habitable have often been overlooked as emphasis has been placed on mechanical ventilation systems and air conditioning to create comfortable spaces that do produce the desired result, but at great cost in terms of energy use.

Alongside the use of these traditional strategies for managing the indoor environment, using traditional materials can promote a healthier indoor environment. The air we breathe inside buildings has become polluted from the effects of a reliance on modern, often synthetic, materials. Synthetics, derived from oil (and therefore not sustainable themselves), are prevalent in many floor coverings, wall coverings and paints; they are also within the resins and adhesives that are used in the production of materials often used in furniture construction (such as plywood and MDF), insulation materials, and so on. Potentially toxic substances can be off-gassed by synthetic materials, and it is these toxic compounds that gradually accumulate in our bodies. Our understanding of the effects of this is not complete, but concerns have been expressed about the long-term health consequences. Traditional paints and surface finishes that predate the introduction of synthetic compounds use mineral or plant extracts that significantly reduce or completely eliminate this toxic element of our interiors.

Synthetic materials

—

Additionally, synthetic materials are generally not "vapor-open"; that is, they do not allow moisture to be absorbed and released, so they trap moisture within the space, forcing it to condense out on wall surfaces, giving rise to high humidity in kitchens and bathrooms and further problems such as mold.

The natural alternatives to synthetics are usually vapor-open materials (for example, clay plasters, wood fiber, hemp or sheep's wool insulation, mineral and natural paints, etc.) and are undamaged as they allow moisture to pass through, thereby regulating the humidity of the interior. Research has shown that these materials are several times more effective at dealing with indoor humidity than mechanical ventilation.

New, more stringent, and ever-evolving standards of building energy performance are employed by architects to manage the energy use within new buildings. In some parts of the world, there is a growing trend for residential developments to be constructed such that they use no additional energy at all for space heating. Instead, these "Passive House" standards (there are different definitions of this standard that go by similar names and that are broadly similar in intent) rely on the heat produced by the buildings' inhabitants during their normal day-to-day activities, by waste heat generated from lighting, IT, TV, and other domestic electrical appliances, and by cooking, to heat the space. Successful examples of these houses can be found in parts of Europe and North America where snow and freezing temperatures are common during the winter, and the external temperatures are uncomfortably high in summer. Unusually high thermal performance like this is the result of careful construction that not only uses increased amounts of insulation but also practically eliminates drafts through "airtight" construction. In these buildings, ventilation is very carefully managed (with much more efficient systems than standard air conditioning), and heat exchangers are used to transfer heat from outgoing to incoming air to maintain the internal temperature. The theories behind Passive House construction might seem contrary to the principle discussed earlier, which referred to a return to simple traditional practices in building design and ventilation, but they do represent another valid approach to the overall reduction of energy use in our buildings.

← Why is sustainability
  an issue?
↓ **Where choices are made**
→ Materials—some thoughts

Building refurbishment

—

Building a completely new structure allows us the opportunity to employ techniques that will provide the best sustainable solution, such as those described above. However, while it is useful to understand the principles, the interior designer is unlikely to have much involvement over what is, essentially, an architect's work.

Working within existing buildings still provides the designer with many opportunities to reduce the energy requirements of that building and improve its environmental performance. In fact, a growing trend is for designers to take the opportunity (where time, budget, and the will of the client allow) to upgrade as much of the infrastructure of a building as possible at the same time as working on new planning solutions and decorative schemes. The vast majority of our existing building stock will still be standing several decades from now, and most of these buildings would allow us to live and work more sustainably if some degree of retrofit was undertaken.

It may well be feasible to utilize many of the sustainable materials mentioned when discussing new buildings above, and so the majority of the sustainability benefits obtained there can also be found in retrofit projects, though the scale of their use may not be so great.

7.4

7.4

The Empowerhouse is a Passive House in Washington, DC, USA. The lower-right portion of the duplex was part of the US Department of Energy 2011 Solar Decathlon, which challenged collegiate teams to design, build, and operate solar-powered houses that are cost-effective, energy-efficient, and attractive.

Generating energy

—

The discussion so far has concentrated on reducing environmental impact through the use of natural materials and also reducing energy use through high levels of insulation, and so on. Most of us will be aware that there are many systems on the market that allow energy from renewable sources (for example, wind, solar, ground heat, and hydro) to be harvested to generate electricity for use in the home, or to heat water directly; many architects and designers are specifying such systems in a bid to improve the environmental performance of their projects.

There is, however, growing concern from some architects and designers that these "environmental fixes" are being applied in situations that are not appropriate and without proper and careful consideration of the consequences. For example, fitting a small-scale wind turbine to a domestic property may seem on the face of it like a good idea, but in reality the vast majority of homes are built in areas where the average annual wind speed is simply not high enough to make these devices work efficiently. Consequently, clients quickly become disillusioned with the technology when it doesn't work as advertised, which in turn leads to a poor reputation for the technology, and there is ultimately a higher cost for the environment than if the technology had not been employed in the first place. The late Howard Liddell, an architect with decades of experience in sustainable design, counseled vociferously against the indiscriminate use of "eco bling," arguing instead for an "eco-minimalist" approach where the basics (insulation, draft proofing, etc.) must be taken care of before any attempt is made to apply green technologies for generating electricity or harvesting energy through other means.

Sourcing

—

If one of the major aspects of an interior designer's role is finding the materials, furniture, fittings, and so on that will go to make up the interior scheme, then it follows that the designer has a lot of control over the choice of sustainable products. There are different strategies that can be employed when looking to source and at the same time reduce the environmental impact of what is being sourced.

One axiom to be adopted when sourcing is "reduce, reuse, recycle." This is an approach that neatly leads to the best possible sustainable result. The designer should always be asking questions about the suitability and practicality of any item or material under consideration for a scheme.

← Why is sustainability
an issue?
↓ **Where choices are made**
→ Materials—some thoughts

07

The items to be considered are:

→ Reduce—Is it really necessary to have as much/as many of this/these, commensurate with considerations of aesthetics and the functionality of the interior?

→ Reuse—Can this material or artifact as it exists now be used elsewhere in this project or on another project? If the designer has no suitable projects of their own, can the material be easily traded or given away via the Internet for others to use?

→ Recycle—If neither of the two previous criteria can be fulfilled, can the item/material be broken down and used elsewhere in some capacity, or can the constituent materials be recycled?

The question of permanence is also of relevance—should the designer specify items that could, in time, become heirlooms? Quality pieces, passed from one generation to the next, will clearly reduce the amount of furniture consumed. Thinking long term can be just as important as ensuring that the client's needs are met in the short term.

Trying to ascertain the environmental credentials of products or materials can be difficult; it is still not as easy as it should be, but this is gradually changing for the better. Enlightened suppliers and manufacturers who don't have anything to hide are more likely to provide information on environmental performance or history, sometimes in the form of a life-cycle assessment that details the environmental impacts associated with all stages of a product's life from "cradle to grave." As this information is usually not independently produced, it is probably best to maintain a degree of healthy skepticism when dealing with these, but they can be useful nonetheless.

Materials—some thoughts

—

The use of almost any material within a scheme is going to impact the environment in some way. Natural materials, such as wood and stone, are used for many reasons, not least because of their looks, but acquiring these materials can put a strain on the local environment.

Stone

—

Variations in the patterning of stone occur wherever these materials are found, and particular variations that are sought for their decorative effect can be extremely localized. Some of the most sought-after examples are now reaching exhaustion in the quarries where they originate and once they are used, they are gone forever. When stone is quarried, it is sawn to size and often polished to bring out the pattern inherent in the material. Both of these operations require large amounts of water to cool the saw blades and polishing machinery.

7.5

← Where choices are made
↓ **Materials—some thoughts**
→ Case study

07

Timber

—

Many hardwoods are also sought out for their decorative qualities. Some highly desired timber species are vulnerable to extinction, and it can be very difficult to be sure of the provenance of much of the timber that is used for construction and decorative purposes. However, schemes do exist that ensure the timber is grown and harvested in a responsible manner; the timber is then tracked to market, ensuring an unbroken "chain of custody" from source to customer. The most widely recognized of these is administered by the Forest Stewardship Council, and timber bearing the FSC mark is available ever more widely. The Good Wood Guide from Greenpeace provides information on the status of particular species and suggests alternatives for those timbers that are endangered in some way, and it can easily be accessed via the Internet.

Plastics

—

Most plastics available today are derived from oil—another nonsustainable resource. Although we dispose of huge amounts of plastic, an increasing amount is being recycled, and products made with recycled content are often indistinguishable from those made with virgin material. Still, many designers will choose to avoid plastics if other suitable materials exist, but sometimes it is the case that plastics are the most suitable in some circumstances—this is a choice on which the designer will have to come to their own conclusion.

Other materials

—

Other materials will have their own considerations—experience will help the designer in determining what to look out for when sourcing, but research may be needed to ensure environmental compatibility.

7.5

The design of this house responds to the surroundings in the use of materials; the façade is constructed from timber taken from the surrounding forest, and the entrance façade reuses steel scrap panels (see also the case study on page 174).

Case study: The Dutch Mountain House, NL

The Dutch Mountain House is located in a rural area of Holland designed by the young Dutch practice Denieuwegeneratie for a family with young children, whose various collections feature heavily in the interior. The design revolves around the idea of the mountain, the interior of the mountain, and the timber canopy, which connects the interior with the exterior—this concept informs the overall design approach.

Denieuwegeneratie designed the house not just as an energy-efficient house but also as a completely sustainable project in terms of energy use, materials, and resources. The design also provides built-in flexibility so that the family can grow and expand into the spaces created.

In terms of energy efficiency, the large glass façade allows the sun to warm the concrete shell, and the thermal mass keeps the house warm in winter and cool in the summer. The wooden canopy regulates sun and is the only visible architecture in the landscape. The open structure of the house allows all of the rooms to be filled with natural light, and this was recognized with a nomination for an International Daylight Award in 2012.

The energy concept incorporates a range of systems using tried and tested technology, which includes low-temperature background heating, the use of the thermal mass to stabilize internal temperatures, and the reuse of gray or recycled water for use in toilets. In addition, photovoltaic panels generate enough energy to run a surplus, and this allows for other uses, such as charging the electric car.

In this respect, the concept of the mountain is carried through to provide a practical means of stabilizing the internal environment and providing an energy-efficient shell for the interior spaces.

7.6

7.6

The kitchen and dining area is a light and flexible space. The airy feel is enhanced by the pale-colored wood. Here, the sustainable elements of the house are celebrated through the materials and the large wood-pellet burning stove, which forms a centerpiece.

7.7

7.7

The interior design of the living space
reflects the interests of the inhabitants
as it contains pieces collected by them.
The pale surfaces and large windows
ensure the room is light and welcoming.

Interview: Denieuwegeneratie

Thomas Dieben is a designer at Denieuwegeneratie a young Amsterdam-based design studio in Holland. The Dutch Mountain House was their first project.

Was the decision to partly bury the building due to a sustainability agenda or planning regulations?

→ The central idea of burying the house was a contextual decision—we didn't want to disturb the open forest plot too much. The regulations didn't allow for a two-story house, but by lowering the ground floor half a level, we could fit in two layers, with the entrance on the highest level.

This is a really striking project and, due to its nature, tends to focus on the interior, which is quite pared back and doesn't feel traditionally "eco." What was your rationale for this?

→ The interior was created as a cave-like open space, almost carved out from the enclosing shell leaving the disposition of rooms, light, and materials mostly flexible, which allows the house to be altered without any issues for years to come. It can still be read in the materials and connective details. The outer shell is kept clean with unfinished concrete; within this, the rooms are defined by lightweight wooden structural boxes with different finishing materials chosen by the clients.

In some respects, the interior seems to curate their collections. Was this an important part of the design process?

→ The clients were strongly involved in the design of the interior. Lucas, the owner, is an art historian and collector of both African art and vintage artifacts. His extreme taste is a reflection of his personality. All we had to design was a house that could work as a canvas for their personality. Many, if not most, of the striking interior jokes, such as the bookcase in a car interior, sprung out of the resident's imagination.

What was your attitude to materials on the project, particularly the concrete, which is not generally considered to be an ecologically sound material?

→ As a material, concrete has quite a big carbon footprint. The energetic advantages it has as thermal mass in an embedded context are actually unrivaled by other choices of structure. This is exemplary for the discussions that were part of this project: what do we consider more important— energy or material? In this case, the energy won since the energetic advantage is a longer-lasting advantage. This is a hard but necessary discussion. It puts the complexity of sustainable design in perspective. It forces you as a designer to take stand: do not try to solve everything at once.

What was your overall attitude to sustainability? Was this dictated by energy performance, low carbon footprint, or recycling?

→ We have tried to insert sustainable thinking in all levels: context, volume, orientation, architecture, materials, installations, and energy use.

Although we started the design with a high-tech attitude, we ended with a preference for low-tech solutions. We recognized during the design phase the domination of energy thinking in sustainable design and wanted to counter it with architectural thinking: flexibility and contextuality.

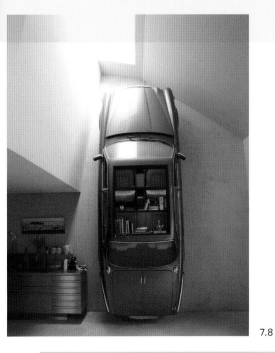

7.8

The interior is both a backdrop and a response to the owner's eclectic collected objects. In this piece, "the car is crucified for its sins against the climate" and is being reused as a bookcase.

7.8

Activity

—

01. Find out what percentage of energy use is typically directed at maintaining a comfortable internal temperature in residential developments in the region of the world in which you live.

→ Is the majority of this energy used to cool or warm the space? Looking at a different worldwide location, how does energy use compare?

02. Find out about Passive House standards. How might these affect what interior designers do?

→ Which retrofit technologies can be implemented easily, and which would require a more radical overhaul of the building structure to implement?

03. What is Greenwash? Why is it important for a designer to be aware of it?

Communicating Design

You know the effort that you've put into the creation of your design. You know how all the different elements are connected, and you've been intimately involved in every aspect of the design. You know how the materials used relate to the concept and to one another. You know and understand how your proposed design solution works. You know all the clever, innovative, and exciting ideas that you have included in the space. But your client doesn't. Having lavished a great deal of effort and time on the design of a space, including research, planning, and sourcing, among other things, the next stage of the process is to share the fruits of those efforts with the client.

This section looks at the different means of presenting work so that it can be easily understood by the client. This is more than a nicety; it is crucial if you are going to engage the client and, ultimately, sell your scheme. If the work that you present is easy to understand and attractively presented, the client will instantly be on your side. If, on the other hand, the work is not clear or the presentation work is not as neat as it could be, doubt is set up in the mind of the client. It may be somewhat irrational and unjustified, but if anything prevents the client from easily understanding the proposal, then it will be harder to sell the work.

8.1

8.1

The illustration of this living room has been created using a combination of SketchUp and Photoshop.

Telling the story

—

The client needs to be educated about the ideas and concepts incorporated in the design. The client needs to be excited and beguiled by your proposals, and as we are dealing with something physical, three-dimensional, and visual, the easiest way to present it is with drawings or models. One of the elements of the design process that has already been heavily stressed during the discussion of design development is the need for drawings, and lots of them, so hasn't the production of drawings and other visuals already been taken care of? Not completely.

The drawings that are fit for presentation are likely to have been taken on a stage further than those that have been used for design development, which would have been accurately drawn but not necessarily finished to a high standard. The drawings used for presentation will be carefully refined and executed in a manner that makes them sympathetic to the style of the project. Which drawings should you use? Those that show the scheme at its best and explain the scheme most fully. How many drawings will be needed to do this? As many drawings as necessary. This is another important point: there is no magic number of drawings that will make the design come alive. Instead, each project will need to be considered carefully to see what drawings need to be made. You will also need to show samples of the materials that are being proposed (real samples if these are available), so that it will be possible to see and feel the actual colors and textures that will feature in the scheme.

Verbal presentation

—

The idea of talking a client through the design in a one-to-one session is something that can make even experienced designers nervous. It is unlike almost any other business meeting. The reason for this is that the designer is so involved with the design that there will be an incredible personal attachment to the work. No one likes to see their work disparaged, particularly when each aspect has been thought through in relation to the brief. However, the truth is that if the drawings and other materials do not provide a strong supporting role to the presentation, then it may be hard for the client to understand the design and see the benefits that the designer is talking about. This personal connection can be used to advantage. It will mean that the designer can be passionate about the work, making for a convincing and compelling argument for its adoption. The presentation will, however, need to be carefully judged as not all clients would appreciate an overly enthusiastic or flamboyant approach to presentation.

The sales pitch

Every presentation is essentially a sales pitch, and the person who is presenting should try to adopt every technique, however subtle and apparently unimportant, to close the sale and put forward a convincing proposal. This applies whether the person (or persons) being presented to is (or are) the client, or the designer's superior who is deciding which proposal to develop for later presentation to the client. These techniques could be summarized as making a good impression and will include anything from being punctual to being appropriately dressed. An appropriate style of delivery can also be important. Should it be formal or informal? This can be difficult to judge in advance but should still be considered; it is a decision made on best judgment.

All of these points matter, and they matter even more if the presentation is part of a design competition. Companies and organizations with a need for a designer may hold a competition to try to generate a number of design proposals from which they can choose. These can be "open" competitions, where an advert is placed in the media calling for entries from interested parties; or they can be closed, where a number of selected designers are invited to submit proposals. Competitions are often undertaken at the designers' own expense, so with no guaranteed payback, it is vital that efforts are focused on the brief in order to produce a design solution that meets the needs of the client; careful note must be made of any constraints made upon the format of the entry.

It will be vital to maintain the interest of those who are watching the presentation. To this end, it is important to rehearse the presentation and to seek feedback from friends or colleagues on how effective it is. When time for presentation is limited, it might be appropriate to verbally deliver only an overview of the project and rely on the presentation boards to deliver the detail during subsequent viewing by the client. If this is the case, then it is even more important that the boards do their job of explaining the scheme in a clear and unambiguous way.

Verbal presentations may follow a fairly rigid format, with the presenter progressing through each part of the design proposal step by step, or they could be more informal, being more of a conversation between designer and client. Although the designer must aim to create as complete a picture as possible with presentation boards, there may be situations that require further explanation. In such instances, it is useful for the designer to be able to sketch out ideas as they are talked through.

Presentation drawings

—

Chapter 3 looked at the use of technical drawings as aids to the understanding of space and the development of a design solution. In particular, plans, elevations, and sections were introduced as the primary methods for depicting the horizontal and vertical planes of an interior. Other drawing types exist that can be used to see the space as if from different, and in varying degrees more realistic, viewpoints. When deciding which drawings are needed to explain the scheme, careful note must be made of the important points that need to be explained. Existing drawings used to aid the planning of the space may be used as presentation drawings, or it may be necessary to create completely new drawings.

Three-dimensional drawings

—

There are two other basic types of drawing that show spaces and objects in three dimensions; the first type uses geometric drawing techniques to create a pseudo 3D effect. However, because they ignore the foreshortening effects that we see in real life, they can look somewhat distorted. They are usually drawn to represent the space as viewed from outside its boundaries. Vertical lines on the drawing represent heights, while widths and depths are represented by lines at other fixed angles. The family name for these drawings is "axonometric," and the two most common are "plan oblique" (where widths and depths are represented by lines drawn at 45° to the horizontal) and "isometric" (in which width and depth are shown by lines drawn at 30° to the horizontal). Perhaps, slightly confusingly, in interior design parlance, plan oblique drawings are often referred to as axonometric, while isometric drawings retain the name isometric.

In the plan oblique or axonometric drawing, the plan shape of any item remains unchanged as it is elevated to its correct height in the drawing. Thus, a circular table, for example, will be drawn with a circular top, which is contrary to our experience of seeing such a table in real life, and so to some extent the drawing looks unnatural. However, it can be a useful drawing because it allows us to produce a basic three-dimensional interpretation of a space or an object relatively quickly. The drawing creates a feeling of viewing the subject from a high viewpoint, and so is helpful when drawing views of relatively small spaces, typically bathrooms or kitchens. The fact that the plan view remains unchanged makes the initial set up of this drawing relatively fast.

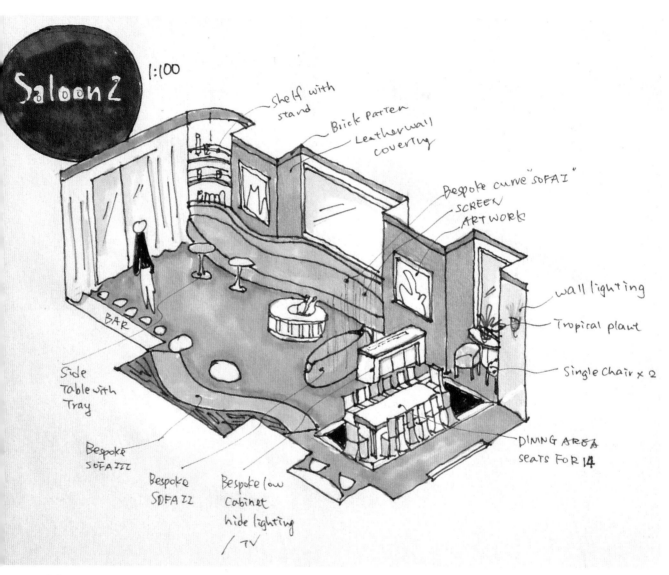

Saloon 2 1:100

Shelf with stand

Brick Patten

Leather wall covering

Bespoke curve "SOFA I"

SCREEN

ARTWORK

wall lighting

Tropical plant

Single Chair x 2

BAR

Side Table with Tray

Bespoke SOFA III

Bespoke SOFA II

Bespoke low Cabinet hide lighting / TV

DINING AREA seats FOR 14

8.2

8.2

This isometric drawing is used to explain the saloon
deck of a yacht. It has been drawn to scale on the
drawing board but traced freehand to soften the
lines and add warmth. Annotations explain the
features of the design, and the figure adds scale.
The drawing is loosely rendered with marker pens.

183

Isometric drawings

Isometric drawings depict widths and depths with lines at 30° to the horizontal, therefore, they cannot be based directly upon an existing plan drawing. A new isometric plan must be drawn, though in reality this isn't such a big task. The angles involved also give the drawings a more natural appearance than the plan oblique, though there is still no use of perspective in the drawing.

The second type of drawing is the perspective drawing. There are formal geometric techniques for creating perspective drawings by hand on the drawing board, and although the results of these drawings can be spectacular they can be very time-consuming to produce. Consequently, many designers will use sketch-perspective techniques to create less formal perspective drawings more quickly, or they might base a perspective drawing on a photo taken of a model of the space, or on a 3D model generated on the computer with programs such as SketchUp.

8.3

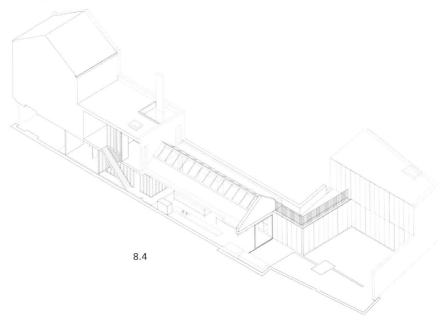

8.4

Drawing treatments

—

The techniques employed dictate the basic format of the drawing, and the appropriate drawing method will be chosen because a particular result is required. However, much of the look and feel of any of the drawing types depend upon the tools used for mark-making and the personal style of the author of the drawing. Different media and techniques should be tried and practiced so that a good knowledge of the possibilities is built up.

Careful rendering (application of color) of the finished drawing will add further possibilities that can add to the effectiveness of the drawings in terms of selling the scheme. Any technique may be appropriate and ultimately, one of the tasks of the designer is to make a judgment as to which style will best fit the presentation. Some of the options are covered below.

Non-rendered line drawings

These drawings focus on the quality and style of the line to communicate their message. Copies of the pencil drawings straight from the drawing board are quick to produce. They suggest a work in progress that could form the basis of a discussion between designer and client about the direction the design proposal is taking. These drawings will probably have quite a cold and unsympathetic but businesslike feeling about them.

Drawings that have been traced in ink using technical pens will feel considerably more finished, but the stark contrast of black on white can make them seem quite empty. This can be addressed by copying the inked drawing onto colored or textured paper stock, by tracing the line work freehand without the use of technical drawing instruments, or by using negative photocopying techniques that turn black on white into white on black—all of which can be very effective. Tracing the drawing freehand provides satisfying results. It generates a visual that is "softer" than one produced using the drawing instruments, and in presentation the effect is much less dictatorial and much more conversational. When using CAD software to create technical drawings, take time to vary the line widths used to represent different parts of the drawing, as would happen if penning manually with technical pens. This avoids the barren look that would otherwise result.

8.3

This well-constructed and well-rendered perspective drawing provides a realistic view of the proposal for a bedroom in a show apartment in China by Chalk Architecture.

8.4

This detailed non-rendered line drawing can be used to explain circulation, construction, views, and a range of other aspects of the design.

Rendered drawings

There are many ways in which shading and color can be added to a drawing. Commonly used media for rendering include: pencil crayons, marker pens, collage, mixed media, and watercolors. Each medium has its own unique feel, and though it is unlikely that an individual will feel equally comfortable using all of these techniques, most designers will comfortably employ two or three as appropriate. Drawings can be fully or partially rendered. Partial rendering naturally takes less time to complete and can be used to focus attention on form rather than finish while still giving an indication of the materials used. The areas rendered could be clearly defined and are of regular shape and size, or they can be more random in nature and can blend seamlessly from rendered to unrendered.

Image-editing software is another means of adding color and texture to line drawings that have been created by CAD software or scanned from manually produced drawings. Several software applications are available that are intended for rendering three-dimensional models produced with CAD packages.

Shaded drawings

A halfway house between line drawings and fully rendered drawings are those that have been worked up to show form through shading only, without the use of color. Pencils or technical pens can be used to add stippling or hatching, and this can produce a very attractive result. This technique can require practice to produce convincing results, but it does allow form to be conveyed without the need for additional media. An even simpler option is to add nothing but drop shadows to a line drawing. With this technique, no effort is made to create realistic shadow effects. Instead, a position is assumed for an imaginary light source (for example, at the top left of the drawing), and shading of even depth and width is added adjacent to the edges of any of the three-dimensional objects that face away from the light source.

8.5

This drawing by Chalk Architecture uses a variety of rendering techniques. The original hand drawing has been rendered using simple color-fill techniques in Photoshop; this has been further enhanced by using scanned digital images, such as the cow graphic, which provides a degree of realism. The visual atmosphere of the space is created without rendering all of the elements, which provides a looser feeling to the drawing.

8.6a–8.6b

These detailed elevations show the proposals for a café concept by Chalk Architecture. The use of simple tones provides depth and interest to the drawings, and the inclusion of furniture and figures gives a scale to the drawings.

8.5

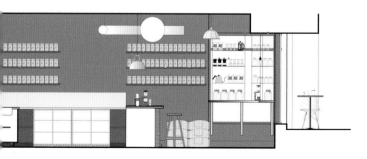

6a

8.6b

CAD drawing

—

At least for some of the time, most designers now eschew the use of manual drawing methods in favor of the computer. This makes sense for several reasons; people are used to working digitally in other areas of their lives, so the production of drawings by digital means is a natural extension of their skills. It also allows changes to drawings to be made quickly and easily, and the exchange of drawings is reasonably trouble free. However, as discussed in Chapter 3, there are those who feel that the quality of the design can suffer when the human connection with the work (through pencil and paper) is lost. Clearly, this is a very personal opinion, but both sides would do well to listen to the views of the other if they are to be the best that they can be. Whichever way you end up working, it is generally accepted that manual drawing is the best way to learn the procedures, standards, and conventions of technical drawing.

CAD software does not automatically produce beautiful-looking drawings that will be an asset to a presentation. In fact, the opposite can be true. The consistent uniformity of a CAD drawing (particularly two-dimensional drawings) can lead to sterile and unsatisfying drawings that are accurate but difficult to read and interpret

8.7a

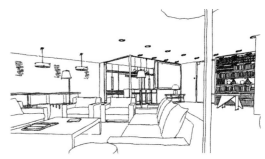

8.7b

8.7a–8.7e

This group of illustrations shows the range of rendering effects that can be created in three-dimensional CAD drawings, from the basic "wireframe" drawing to a near photorealistic rendering. Though some of the rendering effects are not as near to real life as others, they have their own qualities and any one may be the most appropriate rendering style for a particular situation.

8.7c

8.7d

8.7e

Although it is standard practice to differentiate the line weights of a manual drawing by inking with technical pens of various nib sizes, the same effect is often not recreated when drawing with CAD. This is unfortunate as it makes CAD drawings less legible than their manual counterparts, but it is quite straightforward to set the line weights of different elements of the drawing to various values, so recreating the variety of a manual drawing.

CAD programs can be helpful aids to the production of perspective drawings without necessarily being used to create the final visual. The ease with which viewpoints can be moved by dragging a mouse allows the composition of a drawing to be quickly refined. Rough, unrendered visuals can be printed and traced over by hand to allow a varied approach to the preparation of drawings.

Presentation boards

—

All the presentation material that has been carefully generated needs to be organized and delivered to the viewer in the sequence intended by the designer. There needs to be a ready system for ordering and organizing the visuals, text, plans, and other material such that it tells a coherent and easily understandable story. This is usually accomplished through the use of presentation boards or panels. It may be that all relevant information can be presented legibly on a single board, or it might be appropriate to use multiple boards to tell the story (in the context of this book, the term "board" is used to describe any composite of drawings, images, and text that is displayed in either printed format on rigid or flexible media, or digitally as part of a slideshow).

While you may give a verbal presentation to the client in addition to showing a set of boards, it is likely that the presentation boards will be left for the client to review; the client and others who may not have been at the presentation will need to be able to easily assimilate all the material that forms the submission. Once again, clarity is the key as any discrepancies, inconsistencies, or breaks in the narrative of the presentation will create doubts in the mind of the client. Even when the designer has made a verbal presentation, the boards need to be able to stand on their own to explain the design.

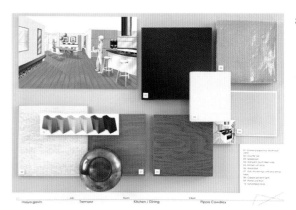

8.8

8.9

8.8

The sample board for this informal kitchen/dining area shows samples that are explained in the key. The visual that accompanies the board has been drawn by hand and rendered in Photoshop.

8.9

Presentation boards must tell the story of the design in a clear and concise way. A lot of care should go into deciding what illustrations to use, which material samples to show, and the layout of the boards. They should be constructed to the highest standards to project a professional image.

Constructing presentation boards

—

Boards can be constructed by traditional paste-up methods, whereby individual images, blocks of text, photographs, and so on are trimmed and mounted onto the presentation board itself; or digital versions of paste-ups can be created in any of a number of software packages. CAD software, word-processing software, presentation programs (such as PowerPoint), photo editing, page layout, and desktop publishing applications can all be used to create digital composites of your technical drawings, illustrations, textual explanations, and product images from suppliers. The digital image can be output to paper for final finishing and mounting or used as an image within a slideshow.

Which is the best route to follow? As ever, there isn't a simple answer; it will depend upon circumstance. Digital imagery can be transmitted anywhere easily, and it has a slick, contemporary feel that can be very seductive. However, traditional methods allow the integration of real material samples within the presentation. Sometimes, there is no substitute for being able to see and touch the real material. Samples of fabric and finishes show depth and character—they allow the play of light to become a dynamic part of the presentation as materials catch the light, and the depth of color or sheen of a surface can never quite be replicated in a photograph. However, they are potentially more expensive to transport and are more susceptible to damage during transit.

Drawings always represent interpretations rather than the empirical truth, but it is important to be aware of the implications of the information that is communicated on the boards. As clients have nothing other than the presentation material to go on, their understanding of the scheme will be derived solely from what is included on the presentation boards. When these are shown in a presentation, they can take on the status of a contract document: what is seen on these boards in miniature is what will be provided on a larger scale when the project is realized. Any deviations or changes should therefore be carefully documented and communicated in writing to the client, and the client will need to be made aware that while every effort will be made to match the appearance of samples of natural materials, it cannot be guaranteed that they will appear exactly as they do on the presentation boards.

The boards themselves are unique, bespoke, creations in their own right. Every project will suggest a different approach to their use and construction, and if they are to do the job of selling the scheme they need to be compiled to a very high standard. When creating physical boards, all the cutting and mounting needs to be of the highest standard, and when working digitally care must still be taken to ensure neatness and consistency of layout. The time spent preparing the boards should reflect the value of the project. Clients will not have confidence in designers who supply dirty, damaged, or carelessly constructed presentation material, and they could decline to take the project further.

Graphics

—

The careful use and application of graphics—logos and company colors, for example—can further enhance presentation material and lift it above the mundane. It is another opportunity to strengthen the visual appeal and impact of the work and to also enhance its credibility.

It is important that logos are of the highest visual quality, and it may be a wise investment to use the services of a graphic designer when establishing the look of a company. It is sensible to establish not just a logo but a complete corporate identity. This can be applied to any presentation material and the need for a consistent house style will drive the creation of templates for word-processed documents, which in turn will speed up the production of project documentation where it is necessary.

8.10

8.10

This student's sample board uses a title block to incorporate the concept images, and it can be easily repeated across a set of presentation boards to help create a uniform look for a body of work.

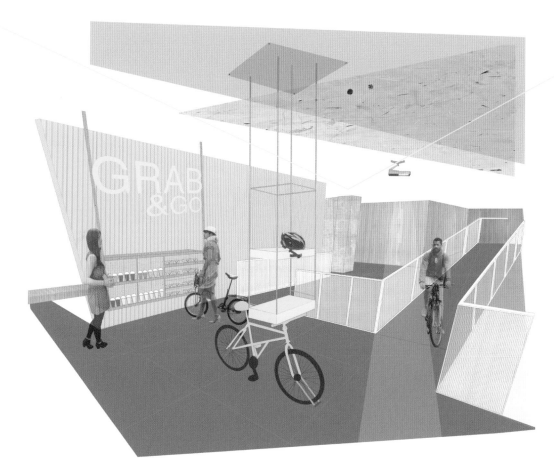

8.11

8.11

Sarah Nevins produced this drawing for her final student project at Manchester University, UK. It has a clear graphic style, which communicates not only the spatial atmosphere but also the graphic language of the space and the identity through the strong use of color and typography. It has been produced using simple fill techniques coupled with the addition of digital images of people and other elements.

Thinking point: Presentation boards

—

If you are to produce compelling presentation material that spans more than one presentation board, there are several aspects that will need careful planning. Before committing to any one method or format, mock-ups will help to identify any problems that could arise.

Construction: As described elsewhere, the construction of the boards can use traditional "paste-up" techniques, or it could involve mounting a single digitally printed composite image onto a presentation board.

Size: When working with physical boards, their size will be dictated largely by the amount of information to be communicated, but the needs of transportation and display should also be considered. Typically, boards may range from the large A1 size (23.4in x 33.1in), to the smaller A2 (16.5in x 23.4in) or even A3 (11.7in x 16.5in) format. Some design competitions require initial submissions to be in A4 format (8.3in x 11.7in).

Orientation: Landscape format is generally more appropriate than portrait, but breaking from the norm can add impact. When using multiple boards, a more effective approach is to maintain the same board orientation throughout. If either the orientation or overall size of any board needs to be changed, a strong visual connection can be maintained by ensuring that one common dimension is consistent, for example, within a series of A2 boards (16.5in x 23.4in) displayed in landscape format, a smaller A3 board (11.7in x 16.5in) shown in portrait format will maintain the flow of the presentation.

Color: The background color of the board needs careful thought so that it supports the other material displayed without overpowering it. Neutral colors can work well, but stronger colors are likely to need strong visuals to justify and balance a strong board color.

Layout: The way that the separate parts of the composition relate to one another is of prime importance. A good layout will allow the eye to move around the board without missing vital information and without stumbling over cluttered composition. Layout is often as much about what is left off the board as about what is put on. Most compositions benefit from careful use of negative space (the space between images, text, and so on). The size of border, if any, has an impact upon the feel of the board. Very generous borders can actually make the content of the board look more precious.

Grids: These are allied to layout and help the designer to visually order and arrange the content of the board. Print designers use grids, and an examination of magazine layout will show that grids do not need to be regular, symmetrical arrangements but instead can be used to create visual rhythm and interest.

Type

—

Type has a major effect on the graphic feel of presentation work, and its use can profoundly change the effectiveness of the boards. The subject of type is complex and worthy of detailed study in its own right, but an appreciation of the possibilities will help when preparing work for presentation. When choosing which typeface is appropriate for a project, reference to the concept should once again provide guidance. While unusual display typefaces can be used for titles or headlines, larger blocks of text will need typefaces that are simpler and clearer if they are to be legible. Type can arouse strong passions in some people, and appropriateness is always the key in its use. Personal likes and dislikes will sometimes have to give way to a considered appraisal of the visual qualities of a particular typeface.

When used on a computer, a particular typeface will only appear as intended if it is actually installed on that computer. Therefore, when transferring data digitally between computers, it is vital that checks are made to ensure that any typefaces used on the source computer are also installed on the destination computer. If this is not the case, a default typeface will be substituted and it is likely that the layout of typographical elements will change, perhaps radically, thus destroying the careful work that has gone into creating a successful layout. This is not, however, the case when layouts are converted into image files, so this could be one course of action to take before transferring files from one computer to another. The downside to this course of action is that some, if not all, flexibility in the layout will be lost in the conversion to an image file.

8.12a

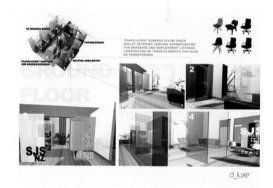

8.12b

8.12a–8.12b

Both of these images form part of a presentation that has been worked up and rendered in CAD. The boards are digital composites of images and text from several sources, which have been skillfully combined to describe the proposal for the space in a clear and unambiguous manner. The resulting image file can then be displayed in any desired fashion and, if necessary, easily transmitted to other locations.

Models

—

Simple models that help the understanding of a
space were explored in Chapter 3. For presentation
purposes, models that have been more carefully
constructed can be used to explain the space to
the client. Unrendered white models will help to
focus attention on the three-dimensional qualities
of the space, and rendered models can be used
to communicate the impact of the decorative
scheme. Models can be physical or digital.

8.13

8.13

Technology has advanced so
that the 3D-rendered digital
model can look very realistic.
Rendered models can be
shown to the client and also
used on presentation boards.

Multimedia presentations

—

Digital technology gives us new ways to present our work and multimedia presentations allow us to create presentations that can be viewed without the designer being present to give a conventional verbal explanation of the design. The usual definition of multimedia is "a software application that can combine text, images, graphics, video, and sound into an integrated package for presentation." In practice, this usually means using software, such as PowerPoint (Microsoft), Keynote (Apple), or Impress (OpenOffice) to create some form of slideshow, though other options do exist (Flash presentations, for example). All three main packages are broadly similar, each with its own strengths and idiosyncrasies.

This type of presentation will still use many of the same drawings as a standard presentation, albeit they will be scanned versions or drawings exported directly from CAD packages. Video can be added in the form of a "fly-through" generated from three-dimensional modeling packages, or from within CAD programs, though care should be taken to check the reliability and compatibility of the selected software before deadlines become pressing.

Soundtracks, such as music and narration, can be added to slideshows, and while this is reasonably straightforward, practice is again important as it can take time to learn the process. The sound-handling capabilities of the presentation software can be rather limited, and the editing of sound files is not generally possible within the software. Capable freeware sound-editing software can be found on the Internet, which will allow the recording and editing of a narration or music track before inclusion in the slideshow.

Before preparing a slideshow, take time to observe professionally made product videos or other slideshows. The most effective use the full capabilities of the software but do so with subtlety. Animations, slide changes, and effects are kept relatively simple and discreet. A restricted tool kit of simple slide changes and animations gives continuity and choice without allowing the presentation to descend into clichéd chaos as distracting animations cheapen the effect that should be created.

Advances in technology

—

Designers are frequently "early adopters" of technology; it's often in their nature to be curious about the capabilities of digital equipment, including technology that provides new ways to get their message across to clients. While laptops will continue to provide versatile platforms for developing, transporting, and showing presentations for some time, the drive to sleeker, lighter, and more stylish equipment on which to display a previously prepared presentation means that tablet devices have quickly proved popular for this job.

What is important to remember is that you will be trying to communicate some important and potentially complex concepts to your client. When presenting to a client, it is important to ask yourself the question: "Am I making myself clear?" If the legibility and clarity of a presentation is compromised by a small screen size, for example, then you will not be doing your work justice, no matter how contemporary the equipment on which you choose to display your work.

There is no doubt that the simplicity of tablet devices can be an effective aid to presentation, but it only works when the content is not compromised. Be ready to change the way you present in order to capitalize on the benefits of new technologies; don't assume that changing the way you work with clients can be done without a significant investment of time and effort on your part. And as has always been the case, when you have an important presentation, there is no substitute for practice, more practice, and still more practice beforehand.

8.14

8.14

New technology enables us to use more sophisticated tools to present and create designs. Here, a designer uses an iPad CAD application to model the 3D layout for the design of a new project. You can see the interior of the house clearly.

Activity

—

01. Look at some online portfolios of designers' work.

→ Does the work speak for itself? Does it tell a story that you can understand?

→ Has the designer chosen the most appropriate illustrations and visuals to explain their ideas?

→ In addition to drawings and illustrations, how much text and/or annotations have been used? Are notes and text written in a way that is easy to understand?

→ Can you determine if all of the work has been originated digitally? Or have manual drawings been transferred to digital media? How has the method of production affected the feel of the presentation?

Bibliography

—

The following personal selection of books has been chosen with the aim of inspiring as well as informing, because learning about interior design is not just about the learning process (though that is a part of it), it's about being passionate and caring enough to create spaces that work. Some of the books illustrate and explain through case studies, some are textbooks, some are essays. All of them can make you think critically about design and about interiors.

Bramston, David. *Material Thoughts*. Lausanne: AVA Publishing, 2009.

Brooker, Graeme and Sally Stone. *Basics Interior Architecture: Context and Environment*. Lausanne: AVA Publishing, 2008.

Brooker, Graeme and Sally Stone. *Basics Interior Architecture: Form and Structure*. Lausanne: AVA Publishing, 2008.

Brooker, Graeme and Sally Stone. *ReReadings (Interior Architecture)*. London: RIBA Books, 2004.

Brown, Rachael and Lorraine Farrelly. *Materials and Interior Design*. London: Laurence King Publishing, 2012.

Ching, Francis and Corky Binggeli. *Interior Design Illustrated*, (3rd Edition). Chichester: John Wiley and Sons, 2012.

de Botton, Alain. *The Architecture of Happiness*. London: Penguin, 2007.

Elam, Kimberley. *The Geometry of Design*. New York: Princeton Architectural Press, 2001.

Farrelly, Lorraine. *Basics Architecture: Construction + Materiality*. Lausanne: AVA Publishing, 2009.

Farrelly, Lorraine. *Basics Architecture: Representational Techniques*. Lausanne: AVA Publishing, 2007.

Fletcher, Alan. *The Art of Looking Sideways*. London: Phaidon, 2007.

Gagg, Russell. *Basics Interior Architecture: Texture + Materials*. Lausanne: AVA Publishing, 2011.

Grimley, Chris and Mimi Love. *Color, Space, and Style*. Minneapolis: Rockport Publishers Inc., 2007.

Hudson, Jennifer. *From Brief to Build.* London: Laurence King Publishing, 2010.

Innes, Malcolm. *Lighting for Interior Design.* London: Laurence King Publishing, 2012.

Liddell, Howard. *Eco-minimalism: The Antidote to Eco-bling.* London: RIBA Publishing, 2008.

Locker, Pam. *Basics Interior Design: Exhibition Design.* Lausanne: AVA Publishing, 2010.

McCloud, Kevin. *Colour Now.* London: Quadrille, 2009.

Mesher, Lynne. *Basics Interior Design: Retail Design.* Lausanne: AVA Publishing, 2010.

Mitton, Maureen. *Interior Design Visual Presentation*, (3rd Edition). Chichester: John Wiley and Sons, 2008.

Moxon, Sian. *Sustainability in Interior Design.* London: Laurence King Publishing, 2012.

Paredes, Cristina. *The New Apartment: Smart Living in Small Spaces.* New York: Universe Publishing, 2007.

Plunkett, Drew. *Construction and Detailing for Interior Design.* London: Laurence King Publishing, 2010.

Plunkett, Drew. *Drawing for Interior Design.* London: Laurence King Publishing, 2009.

Riewoldt, Otto. *New Hotel Design.* London: Laurence King Publishing, 2006.

Ryder, Bethan. *New Bar and Club Design.* London: Laurence King Publishing, 2009.

Salvadori, Mario. *Why Buildings Stand Up.* London: W.W. Norton and Co., 1991.

Spankie, Ro. *Basics Interior Architecture: Drawing out the Interior.* Lausanne: AVA Publishing, 2009.

Storey, Sally. *Lighting by Design.* Hove: Pavilion Books, 2005.

Tanizaki, Junichiro. *In Praise of Shadows.* London: Vintage, 2001.

Online Resources

—

Online magazines

Archidesignclub
www.archidesignclub.com/en

Architizer
www.architizer.com

Architonic
www.architonic.com

Blueprint and FX magazine's online presence
www.designcurial.com/folksonomy/blueprint

Designboom
www.designboom.com/interiors

Detail
www.detail-online.com

Dezeen
www.dezeen.com

Frame
www.frameweb.com

Interior Design Magazine
www.interiordesign.net

Interior design blogs

Cribcandy
www.cribcandy.com

The Cool Hunter
www.thecoolhunter.co.uk

Cool Hunting
www.coolhunting.com

Design Milk
www.design-milk.com

Oblique Strategies; to help overcome designers block
www.joshharrison.net/oblique-strategies

Playing with color schemes
www.kuler.adobe.com/create/color-wheel

Remodelista
www.remodelista.com

Thoughts on retail design
www.retaildesignblog.net

Trend spotting

Trendland
www.trendland.com

Material databases

Materia
www.materia.nl

Materials Connexion
www.materialconnexion.com

SCIN
www.scin.co.uk/index.php

Sustainability assessment tools

BREEAM
www.breeam.org/about.jsp?id=66

LEED
www.leed.net

Professional organizations

American Society of Interior Designers (ASID)
www.asid.org

British Institute of Interior Design
www.biid.org.uk

Chartered Society of Designers
www.csd.org.uk

Interior Design Educators Council
www.idec.org

The Design Institute of Australia
www.dia.org.au

The International Federation of Interior
-Architects/Designers
www.ifiworld.org

Index

—

Picture credits

—

The publishers would like to thank the following for their contributions to this book:

p. 9 Guy Montagu-Pollock/Conran & Partners

pp 10–11 Project Orange

p. 15 Mark Humphrey

p. 17 Stephen Anderson

pp 18, 21 Simon Dodsworth

pp 22–4 Photography by Jim Stephenson

pp 26–7 Sanna Fisher-Payne/BDP

p. 31 Shutterstock.com

pp 32–3 Dani La Cava

p. 34 Natalie Tepper/Arcaid/Western Pennsylvania Conservancy

p. 39 Louise Melchior/Richard Davies/Brinkworth

p. 41 Natalia O'Carroll

p. 42 Project Orange

pp 43, 45–6 Hanna Paterson

pp 48–9, 51 Sanna Fisher-Payne/BDP

pp 52–4 Chae Pereira Architects

pp 56–7 Stephen Anderson

p. 59 KLC School of Design

p. 61 Bokic Bojan/Shutterstock.com

p. 63 Simon Dodsworth

p. 65 Project Orange

p. 66 Sarah Nevins snevins@blogspot.com

pp 68–9, 71 Chae Pereira Architects

pp 73–4 Darryl Sleath/Shutterstock.com

p. 75 Alan Weintraub/Arcaid

p. 77 Stephen Anderson

p. 79 Darryl Sleath/Shutterstock.com

p. 81 Yampi/Shutterstock.com (tl); Project Orange (tr); Ross Hailey/Fort Worth Star-Telegram/MCT via Getty Images (b)

p. 83 Lived In Images/Getty Images

p. 85 Nelson Design

pp 87, 89 Peter Sieger

pp 90–1 Project Orange

pp 92–3, 95 Sarah Tonge

p. 97 Stephen Anderson

p. 99 Based Upon

p. 101 Project Orange

p. 104 UIG via Getty Images

p. 107 Guy Montagu-Pollock/Conran & Partners

p. 108 Project Orange (l); Blacksheep (r)

p. 109 Amada Tuner/GAP Photos/Getty Images

pp 110–1 Sylvain Grandadem/age footstock/Getty Images

p. 112 Jonathan Tuckey Design

p. 115 MSL Interiors/Museum of London

p. 117 Paul Raeside/Conran & Partners

p. 119 Guy Montagu-Pollock/Conran & Partners

pp 120–1 Paul Bradbury/Getty Images

p. 123 Based Upon

p. 124 Based Upon (l); Manczurov/Shutterstock.com (r)

Acknowledgments

—

It's fair to say that this second edition of The Fundamentals of Interior Design is even more of a team effort than the first.

Kate Duffy at Bloomsbury managed to keep the project on track, and did so by bringing Stephen Anderson on board to provide the excellent interviews and case studies. My hope when writing the first edition was that it would inspire as well as inform, and these additions add greatly to the book; they are exactly what nascent designers need to show them what is possible and what they can aim for.

Along the way, various people have provided support, sometimes practical and sometimes moral, and especially deserving of thanks are Steven Separovich, Tina Norden, and Sarah Hazell.

As any textbook is about passing knowledge on to the next generation, I would again like to dedicate my part of this book to my own "next generation": my two boys Chad and Zach.

Simon Dodsworth

There are many people that have helped me with my contributions to this book, not least Kate Duffy and Brendan O'Connell for their support and help, as well as Simon Dodsworth for his encouragement and collaboration.

I would also like to thank all of the contributors to the case studies for their time and patience; there are too many to mention but I hope I have done their work justice.

In contributing to this book I must also acknowledge the support from my colleagues at the University of Portsmouth, especially Lynne Mesher and Rachael Brown for their help and guidance.

And finally, my contribution came at a busy time for me so I must thank my wife Lucy and children Chad and Finn for their patience and forbearance, and I dedicate this book to them.

Stephen Anderson